FRONTIER
FEVER

৩৩৩৩

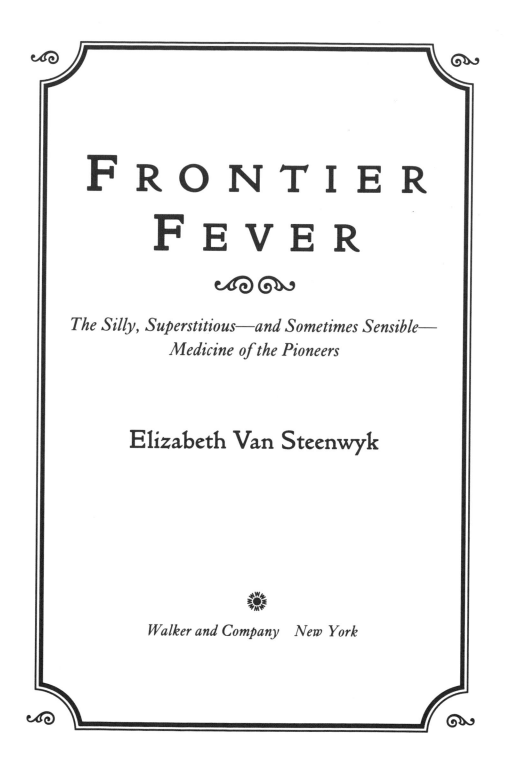

FRONTIER FEVER

The Silly, Superstitious—and Sometimes Sensible—
Medicine of the Pioneers

Elizabeth Van Steenwyk

Walker and Company   New York

First published in the United States of America in 1995 by Walker Publishing Company, Inc.

Published simultaneously in Canada by Thomas Allen & Son Canada, Limited, Markham, Ontario

Library of Congress Cataloging-in-Publication Data
Van Steenwyk, Elizabeth.
Frontier fever : the silly, superstitious, and sometimes sensible medicine of the pioneers / Elizabeth Van Steenwyk.
p. cm.
Includes bibliographical references (p.   )
ISBN 0-8027-8401-1. — ISBN 0-8027-8403-8 (lib. bdg.)
1. Medicine—United States—History—18th century.   2. Medicine—United States—History—19th century.   [1. Medicine—United States—History.]   I. Title.
R151.V36   1995
610'.973—dc20   95-2386
CIP
AC

Printed in the United States of America

2   4   6   8   10   9   7   5   3   1

For
My Three Physicians

KEDRIN

GRETCHEN

JON KEVIN

⊷ Contents ⥾

Special thanks to the librarians at the Huntington Library, San Marino, California, where the research for this manuscript took place, and to the Thursday Night Regulars whose friendship, critique, and enthusiasm made this project so much more rewarding.

FRONTIER
FEVER

INTRODUCTION

Scattering a flock of chickens in its path, the doctor's horse galloped into the clearing. As he neared the log cabin, the doctor grabbed his medical bag, jumped down from the saddle, and in one leap covered the distance to the door, which opened before he had time to knock.

A distraught woman stood in the doorway. "He's in there," she said, fighting back tears.

The doctor glanced into the bedroom. He heard a low moan and smelled the infection. "I'll see to him," he said, and rushed to the bedside of the woman's husband.

The doctor threw off his black frock coat and rolled up his shirtsleeves.

"My belly hurts bad," the patient said. He groaned as the doctor probed, then probed some more.

The doctor turned to the woman standing behind him. "If it's the mortification, it's too late," he began, "but if it's the inflammation, I can fix it."

The doctor dug around in his bag for a scalpel. "Bring me a chicken," he said. "Bring me all the chickens you got."

The woman hurried from the room. Moments later, she was back with a squawking chicken in each hand. He

1

grabbed a hen from her, slit it open from tail to neck, and threw the bloody, still-writhing innards on the patient's abdomen. Then he did the same with the other chicken, believing the warm chicken parts would "draw" the infection out.

Throughout the afternoon, the doctor slit open more chickens and placed their warm, bloody insides on the patient's stomach. By late evening, his pain had eased and his fever was nearly gone. The doctor looked like a butcher now, his clothes bloody and stained, while the heirloom quilt on the bed was strewn with dead chickens. The patient, however, would live.

In a few days, the patient resumed his chores and told his neighbors that the doctor had saved his life. Maybe he had. This was the frontier, and frontier medicine was at work here. No one yet knew the causes of disease, and little about their cures. They only knew when someone lived and someone died.

∽೦ ೦௰

The American frontier began when English colonists landed at Jamestown, Virginia, in 1607. It ended in 1890 when the director of census of the United States announced that an unbroken line no longer separated the settled from the unsettled portions of the continent. All areas of the country had been populated.

A lot of living took place during that time, and a lot of dying as well. Pioneers practiced many kinds of medicine, some good, some bad, some in-between. But as the American frontier expanded, so did the pioneers' knowledge of medicine.

❧ 1 ❧

OLD MEDICINE COMES TO THE NEW LAND

When the Pilgrims crossed the Atlantic Ocean on the *Mayflower* and landed at Plymouth Rock in 1620, they counted only one doctor among the 102 passengers.[1] Many of the colonists were ill when they arrived; all of them were far from healthy. They prayed and fasted while Dr. Samuel Fuller took care of them in the same way he would have in England or Holland. He practiced phlebotomy, or bloodletting, and also purged, blistered, and induced vomiting.

The doctor was familiar with herbal remedies, too. But he used them only if the patients had brought herbs from home, since the Pilgrims knew nothing about the local plants.

Within the first six months of their arrival, forty-four Pilgrims had died. Dr. Fuller looked after the health of the remaining colonists and those who came later until he died in 1633 during a smallpox epidemic.

The beliefs and customs Dr. Fuller followed were ancient, dating back almost to the time of Hippocrates, the Greek physician known as the father of medicine. Although disease had been recognized for centuries, little was known about curing it. In the seventeenth century, European doctors gave their medical attention to the four basic elements, or humors, of the body: blood, phlegm, yellow bile, and black bile. They believed that a perfect balance of these four humors (or secretions) was required for good health.

Because physicians had such mistaken ideas about the origins of the four bodily secretions, their treatments were equally inaccurate. They believed that phlebotomy, or bleeding, aided in the reduction of fever. A fever was supposedly caused by too much pressure in the patient's veins, and bleeding would relieve that pressure. The doctors used purgatives to induce vomiting in the mistaken idea that this would rid their patients of too much yellow and/or black bile. In addition, hot plasters were often used to bring about sweating and raise blisters on the patient's skin in the hopes of drawing out the impurities within their bodies.

The good health of the Native Americans contrasted sharply with that of the frail settlers. It was even something to write home about. In 1642, a Dutch settler in New Amsterdam (now New York) wrote, "All [Native Americans] are well-fashioned people, strong and sound of body, well-formed, without blemish."[2]

After experiencing the first harsh winter in their new environment, the settlers were eager to learn more about the Indians' healthful lifestyle. Nutritional foods that the Native Americans cultivated, such as corn, squash, and potatoes, were soon added to the colonists' diet. More efficient methods of farming and hunting further enriched settlers' meals. Clothing of buckskin and canoes of bark provided additional comfort and transportation. But medicine was something else.

To understand the practice of medicine among the Native Americans, the colonists first had to overcome their old-world attitudes. It wasn't easy. Despite favorable observations of Indian health, colonial doctors and their patients would not easily dismiss, or even add to, their own familiar practices. Moreover, the colonists had trouble understanding that Native Americans' spiritual life and religious beliefs were bound together with their medicine. Indian medicine was not only physical but spiritual; it not only healed and cured but guided, directed, and protected as well.

Although tribal beliefs were as varied as locations and languages of the peoples, there were many similarities. Generally, the practitioner was called a medicine man, healer, or shaman (some practitioners were women); he was honored in his tribe and nation, and second only to the chief in authority. He served as the middleman between his tribesmen and the evil spirits thought to be responsible for disease. Given four kinds of power, he could heal the sick, perform feats of magic, subject others to his will, and enlist the gods in favorable undertakings (e.g., bringing rain, creating a good harvest, or ensuring a successful hunt).

Although he was not all-knowing, the Native American medicine man treated his own tribe's indigenous illnesses expertly. Digestive problems were frequent, brought on by spells of semistarvation alternating with periods of abundance when the Indians grossly overate. Rickets (caused by a lack of vitamin D available in sunshine and fresh food), rheumatism, and neuralgia often accompanied bad weather. Pleurisy, pneumonia, and the common cold were also the results of a harsh climate. Living in lodges or tepees, which were often filled with thick, greasy smoke, led to eye problems such as conjunctivitis (pinkeye). Fractures, wounds, and dislocations occurred as the result of the Indians' active lifestyles.

The Native American was a keen observer and prac-

Na–buash–i–ta, medicine man of the White Mountain Apache tribe, in ceremonial dress. Respected among their tribesmen, many medicine men prescribed roots, herbs, and vegetables, which were highly effective against certain illnesses.
(DENVER PUBLIC LIBRARY, WESTERN HISTORY DEPARTMENT)

6

titioner who used plants that in some way seemed related to certain illnesses (a theory that later became known as the Law of Similars). For instance, snakeroot plants, which had long, twisting roots, were used to treat snakebite. Maidenhair ferns, whose tightly curled fronds straighten as they grow, seemed similar to muscles as they relax, so Native Americans drank fern tea to ease muscle and joint aches. They used lobelia for asthma and prickly pear cactus (which they also cut up for food) to stop headaches, body swelling, and sore throats. Wild garlic was eaten by Native Americans for many years prior to the arrival of Europeans in America, recognizing that it cured the symptoms of scurvy, which would plague white settlers. Other natural drugs that they found in plants were salicin, used for fever and headache, and ipecac, used to induce vomiting. Of the herbal drugs known to Indians who lived north of Mexico, 170 were still listed in the pharmacopoeia of the United States as late as 1985.[3]

Native Americans were familiar with anatomy and sometimes bled patients and performed surgery. Large wounds were sewn up with sinew; splints were made of wood and rawhide. Pleurisy was treated by the Fox and Sac tribes with incision and drainage, much as it was handled by frontier physicians before modern medication.

In their treatment of obstetric and gynecological problems, the Native Americans employed a number of effective measures. Certain herbs were used to relieve discomfort during labor contractions. Native American women often nursed their children until they were about three years old, so the youngsters rarely suffered from malnutrition before that age. A form of birth control was practiced as well: A Virginian noted that Sioux woodland tribes in particular had "an art to destroy conception,"[4] probably involving herbs.

Indian medicine men used herbal diuretics but did not know what caused edema, or excess fluid in the body. Hemorrhage was controlled by pressure and tourniquet. A dose of feathers soaked in warm water was another way to induce vomiting. Although they had no knowledge of the nervous system, they were quick to treat hysteria, often through ceremonial treatments conducted by the shamans, or healers. In addition, it is now thought Indian cures for hysteria included alternating periods of time spent in a sweat lodge (a simple enclosed structure in which heat and steam were produced by a fire occasionally sprinkled with water) followed by plunges in icy lakes. The sudden physical shock was therapeutic as well as cleansing.

Many tribes practiced a form of group psychotherapy. The healers put on masks, hats, and special costumes. Some also wore medicine necklaces, and most carried medicine bags or pouches. Other elaborate ceremonies and celebrations often were performed to thank and praise the spirits who directed their lives and health.

As part of their approach to good health, Native Americans practiced good personal hygiene. "In an age when whites were more apt to dodge a bath than take one," notes historian Wilbur R. Jacobs in his book *Dispossessing the American Indian,* Native Americans were not only hygienically cleaner but healthier because of this one time-honored custom alone.

As the frontier evolved, a new breed of settler emerged. The settlers, both men and women, had been shaped by the harsh living conditions they'd met, by their good and bad contact with Native Americans, and by the lack of central government authority. The only authority was survival. This resulted in independence, reliance on self, and physical toughness.

The pioneer woman and her children were alone in their frontier cabin, isolated from their nearest neighbors by miles of wilderness. The husband and father of the family was far away, hunting and trapping for food and clothing for the winter.

Circling the cabin outside on this particular day, was a band of friendly Indians, brought there by the tantalizing aroma of baking bread. Native Americans had grown to appreciate and hunger for white man's bread. Now the beckoning scent of several loaves cooling inside had brought them to this cabin door.

But the frontier woman had no plans to share and kept her door firmly bolted. Finally, one Indian could stand it no longer and forced open a window, to crawl inside. The woman was ready and struck him over the head with a heavy, wooden potato masher.

It opened a bloody wound on his head which she then treated with a poultice made of squirrel brains and ginseng leaves. When the dazed patient left a few hours later, wearing the poultice wrapped in a cloth on his head, his fellow tribesmen approved of his medical treatment, if not the lack of hospitality he was shown.

Ginseng had been found by Mark Catesby in the early 1700s when he explored the forests and fields of the future Carolinas and Florida. Other therapeutic plants discovered by him were mayapple, snakeroot, and witch hazel. Another that proved to be very useful was given the name "Tooth-Ache Tree" but was never further identified. Described as having leaves that smelled like orange as well as very astringent seeds and bark, it was known and used throughout the area for toothaches; hence its name.

Jamestown colonists quickly learned about tobacco and sassafras, adding them to their medical remedies. Catesby took these plants back to Europe, where they became immediately popular. Tobacco, especially, was promoted in the colonies and Europe as the remedy for any and every ailment, capable of "help[ing] any grief of the body."[5] There was widespread belief that tobacco could cure gout and hangovers, reduce fatigue and hunger, and open all passages of the body. Before long, men and women alike were smoking or chewing and then spitting anywhere they pleased. Foreign visitors began to think of spitting as a national pastime among frontierspeople.

Chewing tobacco was just one of the many personal habits of the early Americans that not only was disgusting but led directly to health problems, such as ulcers, infected teeth, skin infections, and circulatory ailments, problems that would have put most of them in the hospital, if there had been one.

Because it took a long time to cook food in a fireplace people became impatient and hungry and tended to eat food in great, noisy gulps before it was fully cooked. They drank alcohol at every meal—and between meals, too. As mentioned earlier, pioneers seldom took baths. They believed that natural oils on their skin protected them from illness, which could enter their bodies through their pores. They didn't want to wash away the oils on their skin. One woman's comment on bathing: "I bore it rather well, not having been wet all over for 28 years."[6]

The pioneers also used the village streets for sewer systems and turned once pure streams and rivers into breeding grounds for germs and disease by dumping everything imaginable into them. To make matters worse, the early settlers considered fresh air dangerous to sick people and thought most fresh fruits and vegetables poisonous. New York City would ban their sale at a future time.

Strangely enough, many settlers survived. Among trappers and traders who hacked their way west, the only surgical instrument was a knife, and their only medicine, whiskey. Since they were usually young and healthy men anyway, and the virgin land was unpolluted, they had few health problems except for gunshot wounds and muscle sprains. (Borrowing from the Native Americans, they turned sweat lodges into steam baths. They also added herbs, poultices, and teas to their health rituals.)

An uneasy truce soon existed as settlers expanded into the territory of the Native Americans. Wagon tracks appeared where none had been seen before. More and more colonists arrived from Europe, slowly occupying all the coastal lands along the Atlantic Ocean. Ever hungry for more territory, they pushed farther west, stretching the frontier along an uneven line of cabins and tilled acreage bordering the Allegheny foothills. The Native Americans were pushed west against their will, forced to leave the lands of their fathers and to forsake their familiar herbal remedies.

Among the colonists, dependence on Native Americans lessened, and feelings of superiority over them grew. Health and healing became less important on the frontier as hostile feelings festered on both sides. The Indians began to fight back.

∞ 2 ∞

DISEASE HEADS WEST

Disease had traveled west with the settlers as well. Before the arrival of the white man, Native Americans had lived in a relatively disease-free environment. Now, more Indians were dying from white man's disease than from white man's bullets. Native Americans had no knowledge of, and no experience with, the contagion of such epidemics as smallpox, measles, and cholera, which the settlers brought with them. Europeans had only to camp near an Indian village to wipe it out.

Once the Indians understood the idea of contagion, however, they began to take logical precautionary steps. First, they burned the body of the deceased, then everything he or she had ever owned and touched, including property, clothing, and even the lodge in which the person had lived. In several tribes, it was rumored that when a member of a family died from a contagious disease, the remaining members were killed or committed suicide to prevent the spread of the illness to the rest of the tribe.

Smallpox was one of the first and worst contagions the colonists brought with them. It had the power to ruin the health of families and nations alike. In England, Dr. William

Buchan noted in his book *Domestic Medicine* that "few people would choose even to hire a servant who had NOT had smallpox."[1] In other words, if there was a chance that someone could bring this disease into the home or vicinity at any time, that person was not welcome.

For centuries, medical practitioners had tried to control smallpox. The principle of inoculation had been around for a long time, probably starting in China eight hundred years before the Pilgrims arrived at Plymouth Rock. Chinese physicians ground up dried crusts from the smallpox blisters of the infected. Then they blew that powder into the noses of those who had not yet had the disease, hoping to immunize them. Their rate of success was not made public.

Later, in England, inoculation was attempted by transferring a small amount of pus from a pustule of a victim to a healthy person, thereby giving that person a lighter case of the disease. Not only did deaths occur from this practice, but it also spread the disease and so was generally discouraged, later being declared illegal in England.

Cotton Mather, a Boston clergyman, first heard of inoculation from his servant, who had learned about it while living in Africa. In 1721, Mather tried to persuade someone in the colonies to attempt inoculation. The only doctor then living in Boston who had a medical degree refused.

Reverend Mather finally convinced another doctor, Zabdiel Boylston, that he should try. Half of the people in Boston were already infected with the disease. Sooner or later, the other half might become ill. Why not from the inoculation than from a full-blown case of the disease?

There was immediate opposition. It took two to four weeks to recover from the process of inoculation. Most farmers and laborers could not afford to be away from work for that length of time. Since inoculation was also costly, only

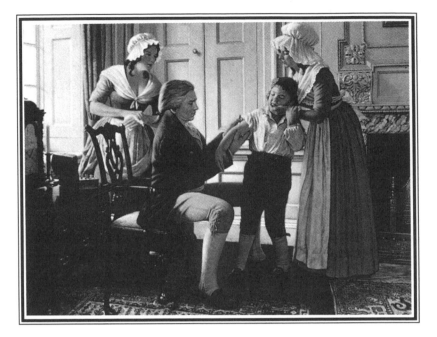

Once Dr. Edward Jenner's vaccination against smallpox overcame religious beliefs and ignorance, children were routinely inoculated against the disease.
(PARKE-DAVIS, A DIVISION OF WALTER-LAMBERT COMPANY)

the wealthy could really afford it. Finally, many people believed inoculation was the work of the devil and refused to take part for that reason. Nevertheless, Boylston inoculated 240 of the citizens, advising them to "drink their Bellyful"[2] of beer should they become ill. The survival rate encouraged Mather and others to keep trying, although no one knew exactly how many members of the community were infected from the process. Later, in 1752, a Boston epidemic was traced directly to inoculation, and eventually New York, Virginia, New Hampshire, and Connecticut banned this procedure.

Smallpox wasn't the only disease to worry the colonists, although diphtheria didn't become a concern until an outbreak occurred in New England in 1735–36. During the eighteenth century, it was impossible to tell the difference between diphtheria and scarlet fever, and so at first they were thought to be the same disease. Their symptoms were somewhat similar. Diphtheria's included redness, swelling, and gray-white patches in the throat, followed by the formation of a membrane over the surface of the throat. Breathing became difficult, and suffocation could follow. The chief victims were children under the age of twelve.

Scarlet fever was considered a milder variation of diphtheria until it became recognized as a separate disease. Its symptoms were sore throat, fever, and red rash. Again, its primary victims were children. No one had an explanation for its origins, although some practitioners thought it might be caused by "Affectations of the Air."[3]

Matters of health were a growing concern in the new nation. Political leaders and formally trained physicians agreed that uniform standards of medical education should be introduced. But no one could agree on methods of study.

Before the seventeenth century, physicians in Europe were considered tradesmen rather than professionals and belonged to trade guilds, often cutting hair, selling medicinal drugs, and pulling teeth to make a living. Tradesmen usually had little formal education, whereas professionals had studied a formal curriculum. Gradually, as medical knowledge began to expand, so did the idea of a medical education. Medical schools were established in London, Leyden, and Edinburgh. It became prestigious to receive a higher education in medicine. This tradition came to the new world with the earliest settlers, although there were no medical schools in the colonies. If he could afford it, a young male colonist who wanted to become a doctor went to England for formal study.

If he could not afford to travel abroad to study, he prepared for a career in medicine in the most popular way then available: serving an apprenticeship to a practicing physician. For several months, the student worked in his preceptor's office, observing, mixing medicines, and occasionally treating a patient. He was also expected to sweep the floors and feed and water the doctor's horse, as well as clean the stable.

After completing his apprenticeship, he went directly from his preceptor's office to his own, hanging out his shingle and declaring he was a doctor.

The majority of the doctors were called "regulars" because they practiced a kind of medicine learned from schools in Europe or from their preceptors at home. It was called "heroic" medicine, whereby health was achieved through the balance of bodily fluids by the bleed–purge–blister-and-vomit method of treatment.

Those physicians who didn't practice "regular" medicine were called "empirics." They lacked professional training and based their knowledge on experience alone. Theory was not a factor. Their first concern was to make their patients feel better and give them comfort. Often they knew a lot about the use of herbs and drugs to comfort and heal. They were generally looked down on by the regulars, and the latter suggested a coat of arms for the empirics ornamented with three duck heads and the motto "quack, quack, quack" printed on it.

Medical knowledge continued to expand despite inadequacies in training and lack of buildings or institutions in which to work. As early as 1717, a pesthouse had been built outside of Boston where patients with infectious diseases were quarantined. There was no attempt to cure the ill, however; the only intent was to keep the patients away from the public. Not until Benjamin Franklin and Dr. Thomas Bond founded Pennsylvania Hospital in 1751 did an institution first serve as a hospital where the ill came to be made well.

There was confusion and dissension over the opening of the nation's first medical school in 1765. Both Dr. John Morgan and Dr. William Shippen, Jr., claimed to be the founder of the College of Philadelphia. Dr. Morgan wanted to provide more Americans with access to a formal medical education, although not everyone was invited to attend, at least in the beginning. He had hoped to found an elite college for physicians, one that would license as well as teach them. Dr. Shippen's idea was to provide more lectures. He instituted lectures in midwifery and anatomy; the latter would give "a few plain Directions"[4] for anyone interested. One year's course work was required after an apprenticeship for an M.B. degree, and three more years of study gave the student an M.D. Few students stayed that long. At first, diplomas served as a license to practice, and the development of formal licensing procedures was sporadic.

Soon, two more schools were organized: King's College in New York in 1768, and Harvard in 1783. Students received training at these three medical schools only through lectures and bedside observations. Little research was conducted. The first human dissections were done in secret because of public aversion to the practice, and the lack of cadavers led to grave robbing. In New York, a mob tried to lynch some students because they had been caught robbing graves. The punishment for this offense was imprisonment and fines. However, one doctor argued that it was not theft since the owner (of the body) had vacated the premises and relinquished all claims! Many of the early cadavers were headless, since their heads had been previously shipped off to dental schools.

In 1771, Dr. John Cochran opened a smallpox hospital near Bound Brook, New Jersey, to care for those who wanted to undergo the inoculation but not the side effects. He had devised a method of preparing future patients for treatment before and after the procedure, which included a vegetarian diet, doses of calomel (a laxative made of mercury chloride), and plenty of rest.

Dr. Cochran's innovative treatment came to the attention of George Washington, who was impressed by the physician's medical ability. But right now, Washington had more compelling things on his mind as war with the British loomed and he became general of the Continental Army.

Medical problems in the army developed immediately owing to lack of organization and authority as members of Congress appointed people to office, then interfered in their attempts to carry out their duties. Dr. John Morgan, called "the unquestionable founder of American Medicine,"[5] by the historian Charles D. Meigs, had been elected director general of hospitals by Congress on October 17, 1775. When petty jealousies and political graft obstructed good medical procedures, Dr. Morgan was forced to resign. His former friend and now chief rival, Dr. William Shippen, Jr., assumed the post, but he too resigned under a cloud of controversy.

Washington remembered Dr. Cochran and took matters into his own hands, appointing him physician and surgeon general of the army in 1777. One of his first duties was to inoculate the soldiers against smallpox. Serving in the army was the first time that many of the brand-new soldiers had traveled any distance from home. It was also the first time they encountered infections against which they had no immunity, particularly smallpox. The disease already had attacked so severely that churches, barns, and private homes were turned into hospitals, with their locations a closely guarded secret from the British. Now Dr. Cochran began to inoculate the American soldiers, three hundred at a time, using his preparation and recovery techniques with apparently good effects.

Smallpox was not the only medical problem of that young army. From general to private, nearly every soldier suffered from poor health through bouts of typhoid fever, dysentery, scurvy, or typhus. Washington, who had smallpox earlier in his life, bore the pockmarks on his face. Now he had frequent attacks of quinsy, a tonsil infection that produced severe pain and high fever. While Dr. Cochran was treating other soldiers, Martha Washington came to camp to treat her husband. She brought onions cooked in molasses with her. It isn't known if her patient ate this concoction or used it as a poultice around his neck. It didn't seem to help either way, for Washington suffered from recurring attacks of quinsy the rest of his life.

At Valley Forge in the winter of 1777, the lack of food, medicinal drugs, clothing, footwear, blankets, and housing took a terrible toll. In his memoirs, Dr. John Hole remembered that during a long, hard march, the soldiers had nothing to eat but "boiled candles and roasted moccasins."[6] Whether or not this is an exaggeration, it still speaks to the severity of the situation.

The British could easily track American soldiers on the march by the bloody footprints they left in the snow. In addition, nearly everyone developed scabies, a contagious skin disease caused by parasitic mites that burrow under the skin. Dr. Cochran isolated soldiers in turn, dosing them with sulfur in "hog's lard."[7]

At the beginning of the Revolutionary War, there were about 3,500 medical practitioners in the colonies. Only about 400 of them had any formal training, and only half of them held degrees. Dr. Benjamin Rush of Philadelphia was probably the most famous doctor in those revolutionary times. A modern thinker for his day, he was a signer of the Declaration of Independence, a crusader for hospitals for alcoholics, and a promoter of public health through his advocacy of clean streets, fresh water, and sewage disposal systems. He also believed in public schools, more education for women, and better care for the insane, who were routinely chained and starved as a course of treatment. He spoke out against slavery, organized the first antislavery society in America in 1774, and wrote many books on a variety of subjects.

Yet Dr. Rush's practices and theories regarding medicine stemmed from the Dark Ages; his methods were all wrong. Quite simply, he believed that all illness resulted from tension in the blood, which could be relieved by bleeding the patient. Lecturing to his students at the College of Philadelphia, he urged them to "bleed, bleed, bleed."[8] Sometimes he removed four-fifths of the patient's blood in the name of healing. Since no one at that time knew how much blood a person had, this procedure was very dangerous. The cure sometimes killed.

Once the Revolutionary War ended, the country was eager to move on as a political entity, writing its Constitution in 1787, electing George Washington its first president in 1789, and conducting the first national census in 1790 to apportion seats to the House of Representatives.

Among those wanting to know more from the census were the country's physicians. Five medical schools were now producing more doctors. New Jersey had established a provincial examination board, and most states followed suit,

Dr. Benjamin Rush (1746–1813) was the most important and best-known person in early-American medicine. Yet his accomplishments in education and politics were far more lasting than his contribution in the medical field.

providing licensing procedures. Regulations controlling apprenticeships also began requiring that the applicant have three years with a practitioner or two years if he had an arts degree from a college. Would there be work for all of these newly qualified doctors, and where was the best place to go to practice?

A general restlessness had developed in the country after the war. When Benjamin Rush noted in Philadelphia that many men "had outlived their credit or fortune"[9] and wanted to move on, he had foreseen a national trend. Before long, more and more Americans were making the same decision, and they all agreed on the direction they wanted to move: west.

But Dr. Rush couldn't go anywhere. Something terrible was happening in Philadelphia.

New Methods, No Cures

Philadelphia was considered a beautiful city of forty thousand in the summer of 1793, but it had no sewage system or water supply. Sewage rotted in the streets, and contaminated water lay everywhere, attracting swarms of mosquitoes. When a yellow fever epidemic began, people blamed it on "noxious miasma," or bad air, and started fires to drive it away. After the fires proved ineffective, physicians suggested gunpowder as a remedy for the stagnant air. Citizens fired their muskets from windows and doorways, wounding many while the epidemic ran unchecked. In addition, women and children smoked cigars, and everyone sniffed vinegar and chewed garlic or kept it in their shoes to drive away disease. Nothing worked.

Meanwhile, Dr. Benjamin Rush worked tirelessly in his hometown, calling on patients and using his preferred methods of phlebotomy, and inducing blistering, purging, and vomiting to overcome their illness. When someone recovered, he said it was a result of his method of treatment. When someone died, he said he had been called in too late to help. More than four thousand people died before the epidemic finally ran its course when cooler weather arrived.

No one knew what caused the disease. In fact, the fever struck so quickly and with such strength that few people had time to react. The incubation period was short, only four to five days at most; then patients developed a flushed face, scarlet lips and tongue, and high fevers. This was quickly followed by vomiting, while the skin turned a yellow hue—hence the name.

The first major outbreaks of what was then called "bilious fever" occurred in 1699 along the waterfront towns of Philadelphia, Charleston, and New York. When yellow fever again struck those same ports during the 1790s, it brought a tightening of ship quarantines. Sanitary reforms were also called for, but came much more slowly.

Dr. Rush and other physicians who practiced heroic medicine came increasingly under criticism. People were tired of continuing epidemics and disease and wanted successful methods of treatment. So far, these "heroic" approaches were not resulting in any genuine cures. Thus when Dr. Elisha Perkins, a well-known and respected physician, introduced his medical miracle that same year, it swept the country like a prairie fire.

Dr. Perkins noticed during surgeries that when metallic instruments were in contact with the patient's muscles, the muscles contracted. He also noticed that pain stopped when metallic instruments were used to separate teeth from gums before extraction.

Leaping to the conclusion that anything metallic would work anywhere on the body in this way, he devised a contraption consisting of two metal rods, about three inches long, rounded on one end, pointed on the other, which were used in tandem. Called "Perkins Patented Tractors,"[1] these instruments were said to extract disease by directing it out of the body. The patient merely had to stroke the afflicted

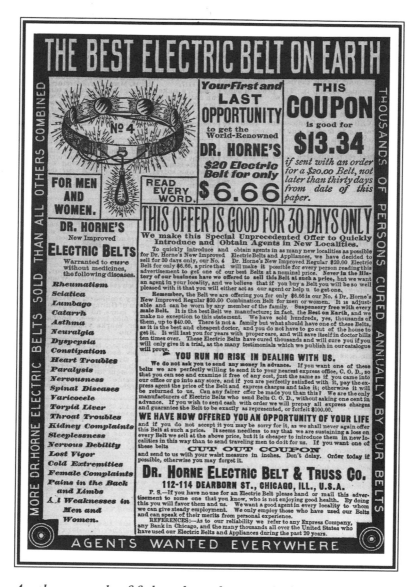

Another example of fad products that promised cures for any and every ailment was the electric belt called "the best and cheapest doctor" by its manufacturer.

(DENVER PUBLIC LIBRARY, WESTERN HISTORY DEPARTMENT)

25

part in one direction with one rod, then stroke in another direction with the other rod and, magically, illness would disappear.

Reports of so-called cures were amazing. Everything from gout, pleurisy, and rheumatism disappeared. One user even claimed to have cured a lame cow. The manufacturer could not keep up with the demand as the craze swept this country and Europe. Even George Washington bought a set. Finally, people realized the tractors neither cured nor slowed down disease, and the mania ended. Nor could Dr. Perkins heal himself when he later contracted yellow fever and died in 1810.

The eighteenth century had seen great advances for the fledgling nation. Now, as the century was coming to an end, so was the life of the nation's first president. In December 1799, former President Washington lay seriously ill. Three physicians hurried to his Mount Vernon home to give him the best care that eighteenth-century medicine could provide. One of the doctors, James Craik, had been personally trained by Dr. Rush and followed his theories of medical practice to the letter.

The three doctors blistered the ex-president, applied poultices, and gave him calomel. They also bled him four times, piercing his skin with sharp lancets and drawing off ninety-six ounces of blood. Nothing helped; in fact, these extreme measures probably hastened his death on December 14 from what was streptococcus infection.

Health and hygiene standards had sunk so low in the United States at the end of the 1700s, they were almost non-existent. The average life expectancy was 34.5 years for men,[2] 36.5 years for women,[3] as infections and disease ran unchecked. Typhoid and yellow fever, diphtheria, malaria, measles, tuberculosis, cholera, and dysentery were ever present. Smallpox epidemics still occurred, but progress was being made against the disease as inoculations became more numerous. Deaths from cancer and cardiovascular disease were virtually unheard of, since no one lived long enough to develop either condition.

Another census was taken in 1800. It reported a total U.S. population of 5.3 million, of which 1 million were blacks. Nine-tenths of them were slaves. A book entitled *Principles of Population* had revealed that the number of American citizens doubled every twenty-three years, and more land was needed to support this trend. Most of the country's leaders, Thomas Jefferson among them, agreed that the United States could support an even larger population if it remained an agricultural society. Out west farmland beckoned.

When Jefferson became the third president of the United States in 1801, he also became chief advocate of the westward expansion movement. The population had to be healthy to settle the West. Medical practices in the United States weren't helping, and Jefferson had long been critical of them, urging that something be done about health and hygiene. From the years he lived in Europe as minister to France, he knew European doctors were better educated. They were also willing to conduct experiments and find answers to serious medical problems.

In England, Dr. Edward Jenner had noticed in his rural practice that dairy workers who became ill from cowpox rarely caught smallpox. (Cowpox is a virus that produces a mild reaction, thereby immunizing the host to a similar yet more dangerous virus, smallpox.) Now he began to inoculate his patients with the cowpox virus, but he called the process vaccination, from the Latin word *vacca*, meaning "cow." The patients then had a case of mild cowpox. Six weeks later, they were exposed to smallpox. They were immune! When Jenner published his findings in 1798, it came to Jefferson's attention, and he began to promote the report in the United States.

Dr. Benjamin Waterhouse was a well-known American physician who had completed his education in Europe. He was more open to scientific experimentation than his locally educated counterparts. After he heard of Jenner's new theory, Waterhouse vaccinated his son, Daniel, with cowpox on July 8, 1800.

To try a new method of medical treatment on his own family took courage and an act of faith on the part of Waterhouse. Yet he must also have known the scientific reasons that it would work. Jefferson sent him a congratulatory letter on Christmas Day, saying, "every friend of humanity must look with pleasure on this discovery."[4]

In 1803, Jefferson negotiated the Louisiana Purchase from France, doubling the size of the United States and extending its boundaries far beyond the Mississippi River. As the negotiations were being completed, he organized the Lewis and Clark expedition to explore this new territory the following year. Captain Meriwether Lewis traveled to Philadelphia to receive special training in botany, zoology, and celestial navigation for the journey. Although it wasn't specifically said, he must also have received instructions in practicing medicine at the same time. Placed in his charge was a large box containing the best medical supplies of that day, including the new Jenner smallpox vaccines. President Jefferson insisted that they be brought along on the trip.

The expedition leaders had been instructed to find a waterway to the Pacific. Beginning in 1804, the company of forty-three men and one woman headed west into areas unknown to outsiders. Lewis and Clark had little knowledge of

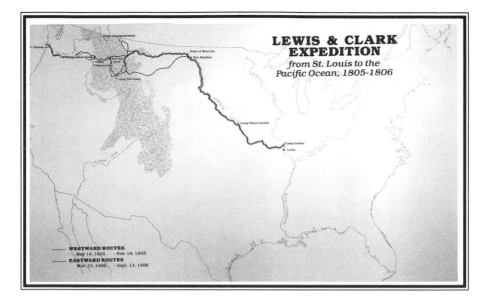

Despite deprivation and hazards of traveling in unexplored areas of the continent, the nine-thousand-mile journey of Lewis and Clark was amazingly successful, and the members of the company stayed surprisingly healthy.

(MONTANA HISTORICAL SOCIETY)

what lay ahead; there were some people who still believed that dinosaurs might live in the wilds of the West!

The trip was successful beyond expectation. That only one death occurred during the three years of exploration is astonishing. On August 19, 1804, Captain William Clark reported in his journal that Sergeant Charles Floyd was taken ill with a condition called "Biliose Chorlick."[5] Lewis and Clark attempted several times to relieve his symptoms, but he continued to grow weaker and died of what was probably a ruptured appendix. Being on the trail had little to do with hastening his death, however. In that day, the condition would have been fatal even if he had been at home.

29

During the expedition, only one serious accident occurred. Peter Cruzatte was blind in one eye but nevertheless
considered to be one of the company's best hunters. One
day, as he and Lewis were hunting for elk, Cruzatte acciden-
tally shot Lewis in the left thigh. Lewis later reported that
"the stroke was very severe";[6] but he dressed it himself,
applying poultices of Peruvian bark until the wound healed.
Lewis considered himself fortunate that neither bone nor ar-
tery had been touched by the rifle ball.

On February 11, 1805, Sacajawea, the Native American
wife of Touissant Charbonneau, one of the official interpret-
ers traveling with the expedition, was expecting her first
child. Her labor had been long and difficult. Finally, she
asked for a piece of dried rattle from a rattlesnake. Lewis had
some rattles, which he then ground up and Sacajawea ate.
Within ten minutes, she had delivered a healthy baby boy.
As Lewis stated in his journal, "Whether this medicine was
truly the cause [of delivery] or not I shall not undertake to
determine."[7]

Both Lewis and Clark spoke of treating other members
of their company for such problems as pleurisy, rheumatism,
and frostbite. Captain Lewis removed the toes of a boy who
was frostbitten and treated a Mandan chief for snow blind-
ness. Many Native Americans were given smallpox vaccinations. Captain Clark also reported treating other Indians they
met on the trail. In his own camp, Sacajawea's case of either
severe indigestion or menstrual cramps was considered
somewhat dangerous until he gave her "the bark" (probably
Peruvian bark used as a poultice). When he applied it to her
lower abdomen, or "region," she revived.

Charbonneau and Sacajawea's small son, Pompey, gave
the company some anxious moments in May 1806 when he
was brought to Lewis with a swollen jaw and throat. The

captain treated the condition with a poultice of onions and cream of tartar. Despite constant applications of the poultice, the child's condition worsened, and finally they placed him in a sweat hole for treatment.

A hole, three feet in diameter and four feet deep, was dug in the earth. A fire was started to heat the hole, then the fire was removed and a seat placed in the hole for the patient. Willow poles were bent over the hole and several blankets thrown over them to completely cover the patient sitting in the hole. The patient was provided with water to sprinkle on the sides and bottom of the hole to create steam, which was considered good for the health problem. Sweat baths or similar remedies were used by pioneers for a variety of medical problems.

A week later, the little boy seemed better, although Lewis thought the swelling on the side of his neck would (and did) result in an abscess below the ear. Two weeks after the child's illness began, he recovered, but not before Lewis made a salve of resin from the long-leafed pine, beeswax, and bear's oil, which was then applied to the abscess.

Both leaders were ill during the trip, mentioning high fevers, chills, and constant aching in all muscles as well as bouts of dysentery. Nevertheless, they continued on their routes, hiking, canoeing, riding horseback, and hunting in a strenuous manner, oftentimes under dangerous conditions. Seldom did they consider themselves too ill to go on with the journey. Only once, Clark couldn't walk because of a "rageing fury of a tumer on my anckle musle."[8]

As the geographic frontier was being probed by Lewis and Clark, the medical frontier was advancing, too. In 1809, Dr. Ephraim McDowell became a medical pioneer when he performed the first abdominal surgery in the nation. While friends and relatives of the patient waited outside her rural

This thirty-six-inch model of Lewis, Clark, and Sacajawea was designed by Charles Russell, sculpted by Henry Lion, and cast in bronze as a gift from Charles S. Jones. It is on display in the Montana Historical Society Museum.

(MONTANA HISTORICAL SOCIETY)

❧ ❧

Kentucky log cabin with rope in hand, Dr. McDowell removed a twenty-two-and-a-half-pound tumor from the woman's abdomen. The surgery was done without anesthetic or antiseptic measures, since little was known about them at the time. The rope wasn't used either; the patient recovered completely, so there was no reason to hang the doctor.

Dr. Rush died in 1813, probably of pneumonia and tuberculosis, after asking his physician to bleed him during his final hours. After his death, Jefferson said of him, "I was ever opposed to my friend, Rush, whom I greatly loved, but who has done much harm, in the sincerest persuasion that he was preserving life and happiness all around him."[9]

Although many laymen disapproved of these harsh treatments, they continued to be used since the majority of practitioners believed the methods had foundations in nature's laws. Calomel was later discovered to be poisonous, yet it continued to be used as a laxative. The side effects were bleeding from the gums and intestines, and terrible sores on tongue and cheeks. Bleeding continued as a remedy since it was considered more practical than the application of leeches, which was a method formerly used. Physicians thought that leeches were not completely reliable because no one knew how much blood the creatures drained from their hosts. The fact that the doctors themselves often didn't know how much they bled from the patients seemed to matter very little.

The influence of Native American medicine remained strong on neighboring white settlers. The Indian medicine men, sometimes called "yarb and root" doctors because of the herbs and plants they used from forests and gardens, had other medical procedures as well. They relied on sweatings, rubbings, incantations, ghost shootings in the night, and

33

*This 1639 graphic depicts the use of blood-sucking leeches once
commonly used to bleed patients. Leech therapy has been
reintroduced in modern-day medicine for
certain restricted applications.*

sucking out of evil spirits. French explorers seemed to prefer
them to white doctors.

Even white pioneers sometimes practiced Indian medicine as an avocation, and they were preferred over some
"regulars." Ads placed in the newspapers told of their availability. T. J. Luster advertised that he was an Indian and
German root doctor who could cure just about anything.

Another root doctor, Thomas J. Chinn, noted in his ad that he lost only nine patients in one week.

The Appalachian Mountains were now no longer a geographic barrier as settlers moved over rough trails into the Ohio and Mississippi River Valleys. But the threat of attack by Native Americans continued, angered as they were by the encroachment of whites onto their land. Territorial expansionist leaders in Congress began to badger the new president, James Madison, saying that the Indians were being encouraged in their hostility by the British. The leaders demanded action against their old enemy and, finally, President Madison was persuaded. The young nation again went to war against England.

❧ 4 ❧

NO OUNCE OF
PREVENTION HERE

American medicine was directly affected by the European naval blockade in the years preceding and during the War of 1812. Merchant ships, whalers, and naval ships had few doctors, so the sailors were bringing home new and different diseases from foreign ports. In addition, the blockade was keeping European drugs away from the Americans, who still depended on them. Depended upon them too much, according to Dr. Thomas Ewell, who felt that someone in this country should come up with a medicine to give "tone or strength to debilitated persons without the aid of peruvian bark, wine or foreign medicine."[1] But if someone had such an elixir, he didn't come forward with it.

Medical records were incomplete at best during the War of 1812, yet out of the confusing data, one clear fact emerged. Wherever large numbers of patients were placed together, in camps or hospitals or recovery areas, more disease and epidemics were the result. European doctors, the French in particular, had begun studies about the spread of disease, implying that tiny organisms called animalculae were transmitted from one person to the next. American doctors were unsure of this new theory, and the American public grew more unsure of the physicians. Individuals relied even more on themselves or others who practiced medicine without a license or diploma.

The Thomsonians were the most numerous. They were named for Sam Thomson, a New Hampshire farmer who blamed heroic methods for his mother's death. He became an herbalist and in 1813 patented his plan, which quickly caught on with a health-hungry population.

Comparing the digestive system of a human being to a stovepipe, he believed that good health could be achieved through the natural powers of herbs alone. His favorite herb was lobelia, a powerful emetic long used by Indians to induce vomiting. He believed that hot steam baths, cayenne pepper enemas, and induced vomiting would soon restore his patients to good health.

Not all followers used his methods to the letter, however. One Thomsonian treated a child ill with measles by placing onions under her arms and her feet in hot water. She recovered in spite of the treatment.

Although medicine had made few advances during the war years, a new spirit of nationalism emerged at the close of the War of 1812. The desire to occupy all the land from the Atlantic to the Pacific soon became an epidemic of its own. The spirit of the Native Americans had been broken in the Midwest. Now they could no longer hold back the avalanche of white settlers heading west.

New advances in transportation helped the westward movement. Ground was broken for the Erie Canal on July 4, 1817. Workers were quickly hired and lived crowded together in large shacks. They were well fed but worked hard, often fourteen hours a day. By nighttime, the rough beds in those shacks were a welcome sight. But there was no glass or screens on the windows of the rooms where the workers slept. So mosquitoes from nearby bogs and ponds drifted in all night long, carrying disease with them.

The disease carried by the mosquitoes was called canal shakes by the workers, but it was actually malaria. As many as one-third to one-half of the workers were ill at the same time. It was reported that, occasionally, the only sound in camp would be the clicking of workers' teeth as they shook from the chills brought on by the disease.

Mosquitoes like to bite in the daylight, too, so laborers devised smudge buckets to hang around their necks as they worked. The vile-smelling smoke from the burning twigs inside the small pails drove away mosquitoes but also infected eyes and noses. No one thought to clear away the ponds and bogs that attracted the *Anopheles* mosquitoes, which transmit the malarial parasite to human victims.

In treating malaria, the doctors of that day did their best. They bled the patients, then gave them concoctions of herbs along with something called Seneca Oil, which was nothing more than kerosene. One bright spot came out of the attempted cures, however: Physicians now began to look for other ways to control malaria. One experimented with "Peruvian or Jesuit's bark" as a possible remedy for malaria's severe effects. The bark came from the cinchona tree, which grew in South America, was taken to Europe by Jesuit priests, and was brought to the United States by Europeans.

Settlers heading into new territory wanted to know more about the areas in which they would be living. What was the physical environment like and what effect would it have on their health? Those who had good health didn't want to lose it. Those who didn't have it sought fresh air, unpolluted water, and sunshine as cures for what ailed them.

Many colonists had previous experience in settling in one place, then moving on to another. They knew firsthand of the "seasoning" period that must be endured before life could become normal once again. "Seasoning" was a period of becoming accustomed not only to the climate but to the vegetation and infestation local to the area. Allergies and the many fevers of the day were the most common illnesses. They could be mild—or deadly.

Pioneers prepared as much as possible for the seasoning period. They had practiced botanical medicine for many years in their old homes. Housewives had learned to gather domesticated and wild herbs, then hang and dry them for future use. When illness struck, they turned to home remedies made from herbal ingredients that they had copied into cookbooks, Bibles, and journals. These "recipes" had also come from newspapers, almanacs, neighbors, and friends, and they even exchanged them with other families they met along the trail. But other remedies ran the gamut from commonsense to bizarre, from ridiculous to hysterical.

Some people believed that colds could be prevented by wearing garlic or placing an onion in the window, providing one had a window. Onions, especially, were the vegetable of choice for treating just about anything and could be worn, eaten, or used as decoration to ward off disease and epidemic. Steam was recommended for nasal and bronchial congestion and is still effectively used today, along with antibiotics. In pioneer days, however, steam was used with a concoction of gunpowder and milk to be ingested at regular intervals. Sore throats were easily treated by wrapping the patient's neck with a dirty sock, still warm from the wearer's foot!

A few practical remedies showed rare insight in treating medical problems. Egg whites formed a sterile coating on burns and cuts; flour or cobwebs slowed bleeding from minor wounds, and kerosene and turpentine had disinfectant qualities. But many remedies worked because the patient would have recovered anyway. Burying a dishrag, for instance, had no effect whatsoever on ridding a patient of warts!

The frontier compounded most medical problems. Along with their hopes and dreams from the old world, the settlers had packed disease. Now they brought it in their wagons or saddlebags as they headed into new territory. One of the most persistent was malaria, which was made all the more virulent by African strains carried by black people brought here as slaves. Known variously as ague, the fever, quartan, tertian, and intermittent fever, malaria eventually traveled all the way west to California, and as far north as Wisconsin and Minnesota.

Pioneers usually settled by bodies of water. They needed water to drink and bathe in, as well as for transportation. As they moved west, the pioneers showed little understanding of the Native Americans' reverent attitude toward land and wildlife. The Indian philosophy of "leave no trace"[2] through the wilderness was lost on the white man.

Now, as settlers began to farm and trap along the Wabash and White Rivers of Indiana and Illinois, they turned the water putrid with their careless dumping of garbage and refuse. In addition, small towns grew so quickly, there was not adequate time to set up sewage systems.

Soon, infestation of malaria was everywhere. Gershon Flagg of Edwardsville, Illinois, must have gone through at least one period of seasoning when he wrote in a letter that "the principal objection I have to this country is its unhealthiness. The months of August and September are generally very sickly."[3]

Called the "dog days" since ancient times, late summer is the season when the Dog Star becomes visible in the heavens. It is also the season associated with many illnesses. Bilious fever was a severe gastrointestinal infection that was most common at the end of summer. So were typhoid fever, erysipelas (an infectious bacterial disease characterized by inflammation of the skin), and the ever-present forms of malaria.

Settlers not only in Indiana and Illinois but in the neighboring states of Ohio and Michigan were affected by disease as well. The autumn of 1819 became forever known in history books as "bad autumn," when fevers and chills hit many midwestern residents living on bottomland along rivers. Over half of the residents within a fifty-mile radius of Columbus, Ohio, were documented to be seriously ill.

In Michigan, pale, sallow, bloated faces were the rule. If settlers appeared to have healthy faces, it meant they had recently arrived from somewhere else. A common rhyme repeated along western trails was:

> *Don't go to Michigan, that land of ills:*
> *The word means ague, fever and chills.*[4]

Ague seemed to be the most common name given to malarial fever, which was endemic—a disease localized to an area. In fact, people were stricken with malaria so often that after a while, they stopped counting it as an illness. "He ain't sick, he's only got the ager"[5] was a saying that made the rounds.

Symptoms were yawning, stretching, weariness, blue fingernails, and cold sensations that caused the patient to shake like a small earthquake, as one observer noted. Then the patient was consumed with a raging fever and severe head and back pains. In most cases, the patient returned to normal until the next attack. As one sufferer described an

41

episode, "You was partially raveled out." Some patients, however, were so weakened by the disease, they eventually died from some other ailment.

In Michigan, cabins were said to shake with ague patients inside, infected cows leaned against fences and shook, and babies were born with it. In the meantime, work and school schedules were arranged to fit the fever attacks. Ministers planned their services and sermons around their illnesses as well as those of their parishioners, and the local judge scheduled hearings in court before or after his and the accused and accuser's bouts.

Some progress was being made against the disease when settlers began to blame filth in the streets, lakes, and streams for causing their illnesses. However, they had yet to discover that the filth was only an indirect cause, as it attracted the mosquitoes who were the real culprits.

All illnesses did not result from infestation. Milk sickness originated with cows who had eaten white snakeroot, a poisonous plant that grew in abundance at the end of summer in midwestern meadows. Pioneers often let their cows out to forage on the waist-high plants, not realizing the potential danger. Within days, the cattle developed "the trembles" and died shortly thereafter.

Settlers quickly blamed the illness on the water cows drank rather than the forage they ate. No one thought to rid the meadows of snakeroot. Meanwhile, the sick cows were an omen of things to come for the pioneers. Once they drank milk from cows who subsequently became ill, the pioneers developed symptoms of dizziness, nausea, vomiting, stomach pains, intense thirst, and a foul breath odor. Settlers then knew what was ahead. Wills were written; families were called to bedsides; good-byes were said. A few victims lingered on the brink of death for weeks before recovering, but most died, usually within a week.

From 1820 on, seasoning reports began to come from a new source as more military medical men were sent to forts and outposts in the new territories. In their free time, the military doctors studied the geography and botanical resources of the area where they were stationed and their possible impact on western settlers. For instance, was the growing season long or short? Would too much rain, or too little, influence children's health, the birthrate, the mortality rate? What kind of herbs grew locally? Were they known to have medicinal value? Reports by these doctors soon circulated among the population by newspaper and word of mouth, and influenced colonists' decisions on heading west.

ᴄᴅ 5 ᴇᴅ

ALONG CAME CHOLERA

Doctors moved west with the settlers, but their numbers were few and their skills questionable. The better-educated physicians remained in the East, in cities where they had growing practices and decent incomes, where hospitals were emerging, and where more medical schools and associations were forming.

The early part of the nineteenth century was not the best time to be a member of any profession, however. A suspicious attitude against all professions had arisen from the egalitarian, or equality-minded, spirit of Andrew Jackson's presidential election in 1828. He and his followers emphasized the value of the common man and deemphasized anything that would show elitism, even in vocations. "We go for free trade in doctoring," the *Daily Times* of Cincinnati, Ohio, proclaimed in its pages; "reason and public opinion . . . [are] sole legislators of the medical profession."[1]

Even the former president of Yale University was contemptuous of the profession of medicine, characterizing medical students as "too weak for the farm, too indolent for labor, too stupid for the law and too immoral for the public."[2]

More physicians or would-be doctors began to practice

*Army surgeon Dr. John E. Bacon and his staff enjoying a moment
of fun and respite from their duties at Fort Grant, Arizona
Territory, in the late 1880s.*
(SPECIAL COLLECTIONS, UNIVERSITY OF ARIZONA LIBRARY)

alternative kinds of medicine, also called sects. One of the
largest groups of doctors turned to homeopathy, begun by
Dr. Samuel Hahnemann in Germany in the late 1700s and
brought to the United States by immigrants. Horrified by
what he had learned in medical school and later saw being
practiced, Hahnemann developed his own theory based on
some ancient teachings of Hippocrates. He then offered a
Law of Similars of his own, saying that a given disease
should be treated by medicines that will produce symptoms
similar to the disease's symptoms in healthy persons.

Experimenting on his own body, Hahnemann gave himself small doses of quinine twice a week. On each occasion, he developed a fever and its symptoms lasted for several hours. He concluded that quinine should be used to combat real fevers caused by the illnesses that produced them. This theory bore a distinct relationship to the Law of Similars that the Native Americans had practiced for centuries.

Hahnemann went on to introduce another theory, that drugs should be given in the smallest doses possible, believing that the smaller the dose, the greater the effect.

Although homeopathy was treated as quackery in its early days, it quickly became popular because it contrasted with the harsher methods of treating the ill used by the so-called regular doctors. Always maintaining a certain professional standing, homeopathy is still an acknowledged form of treatment today, especially in Asia and Europe.

Eclectic medicine became an alternative to every other form of alternative medicine. It had begun in 1820 when Wooster Beach, a medical school graduate, turned to many sources and mixed all the theories together. Basically, his followers copied the heroics' use of phlebotomy, blistering, purging, and vomiting, replacing regular or usual drugs with others that had the same effect.

Despite the increasing suspicion of its practices, the medical profession continued to grow. By 1830, twenty-two new medical schools were in business, and 6,800 new doctors would be looking for work in the coming decade. No wonder doctors were encouraged to head for the West. Soon there wouldn't be enough patients for all the graduates in the settled parts of the nation.

But there weren't enough patients out west, either, so the practice of medicine was not a full-time job. In between patients, doctors had to find other, more lucrative forms of

*Kansas Medical College of Topeka was one of the many
unregulated schools that suddenly sprouted like prairie weeds in
the 1800s during westward expansion.*
(KANSAS STATE HISTORICAL SOCIETY)

employment, such as farming, selling real estate, or banking. Occasionally, it happened the other way around, as in the case of a certain shoemaker. Described as a fellow with a "worsted cap and great black fists,"[3] he happened to cure a local woman of a terrible disease. With that act, he acquired the reputation of a physician, and people began coming to him with their ailments. Before long, he laid aside his cobbling business and took up the practice of medicine full-time, finding it more profitable than shoe repair.

Traditionally, Americans became concerned about illness only after it occurred. Physicians, in frontier days, were expected to restore health rather than preserve it. But now there was disturbing news from abroad that caused concern among the nonmedical population and medical practitioners alike. For the first time in the nation's young life, its citizens began to worry about a serious, life-threatening disease *before* they got sick.

Prior to 1817, there had been no cholera epidemics outside the Far East. But with advancements in transportation and trade, cholera, a severe intestinal infection, began to travel on the same lanes of commerce that brought foreign goods to Western lands. Slowly, steadily, it marched across Russia, then Poland, then the rest of the European continent.

In the United States, newspapers and periodicals, lecture halls, taverns, and churches echoed the talk of troubled citizens about problems closer to home. Indian hostilities on the frontier, tariff disturbances abroad that sent prices soaring in the United States, and questions of bank failures on Wall Street had captivated the attention of Americans in the fall and winter of 1831–32. Then, even more troubling news arrived, and its headlines pushed all others off the front pages. Cholera had broken out in England!

During the fall of 1831 and early 1832, American newspapers, magazines, and pamphlets reported regularly on cholera's spread in Europe. By July, there were few periodicals that had not published at least one article on this disease, urging the government and its leaders to take action.

Medical commissions from the States studied English and French reports, hoping to find a remedy to prevent the disease from moving across the ocean. Restrictions had been placed against travel and trade at European ports, and quarantines were enforced at American points of entry. As citizens read, prepared, and prayed, and the government tried to decide on a course of action, cholera came steadily closer, until it landed at the country's borders and shores.

In 1832, the idea that disease was caused by something

specific, such as a virus or bacteria, was not generally accepted. Rather, most people felt disease was something most often brought on by the patients themselves. Pious citizens believed that cholera attacked only those who had weakened themselves through overeating, intemperance, sinful habits, or panic. Religious leaders urged their followers to be pure in thought and their bodies would follow. However, it was acknowledged that some sinners also lived in this country, especially in New York City, so the nation might not escape untouched.

New York City was the largest city in the United States, and also the filthiest. Its population of 250,000 was not pleased with the thousands of swine who roamed the streets, acting as scavengers. But the Common Council, the city's governing body, remained indifferent, offering little control over the pigs, goats, and dogs who "worked" as street sweepers.

Finally, a law was passed requiring citizens themselves to clean the sidewalks and streets in front of their own homes or businesses. They swept debris into a pile on each block, to be collected later, by the city. Municipal services were seldom carried out, however. Citizens soon called the growing piles of garbage "Corporation Pie, after their nickname for the city, "The Corporation."

City water, available at corner street pumps, was so dirty that only the poorest people drank it. Pure springs and wells in the nearby countryside provided water for those who could afford to have it delivered to them. But the population didn't seem to use much water anyway, since they still didn't bathe very often or wash their food. Although a Board of Health existed, it met only occasionally, and none of its three employees were doctors or practitioners.

In early June, Mayor Walter Browne attempted to halt

infestation by proclaiming a quarantine against all European and Asian trade. On June 13, the city finally enacted a new street-cleaning method, but it was too little and too late. Two days later, word arrived through passengers traveling on an Albany steamboat that cholera had struck Montreal, one of Canada's largest cities. Finally, New York's Board of Health met to enact a plan. City councilmen were to serve as health wardens for their own wards, and five special cholera hospitals were organized. But no one wanted to live near them. The board also offered a reward to anyone who could come up with a cure for cholera.

On Sunday, June 17, every minister in the city preached about cholera. In the days that followed, newspapers printed "cholera extras" with hundreds of ads for medications in them. Camphor, a product thought to purify the air, had doubled in price since the outbreak of the disease. A special medical council published the following in newspapers and pamphlets.

> *Be temperate in eating and drinking*
> *Avoid crude vegetables and fruits*
> *Abstain from cold water, when heated;*
> *and above all, from ardent spirits and if habit have*
> *rendered it indispensable, take much less than usual.*
> *Sleep and clothe warm*
> *Avoid labor in heat of day*
> *Do not sleep or sit in a draught of air when heated*
> *Avoid getting wet*
> *Take no medicines without advice.*[4]

The city's physicians met to suggest plans for public and private hygiene. They urged city officials to wash the streets several times a week and advised the people to remain calm

A garbage dumping ground at the foot of Beach Street in New York City during a cholera epidemic only served to spread the disease as people scavenged through it for food.
(NATIONAL LIBRARY OF MEDICINE)

and keep clean. Many chose to leave the city, however. Since cholera had struck only large, dirty cities thus far, it was thought the clean, country air would be safer. Before they left, the people stocked up on what they believed to be cholera preventives and took them along, just to be safe. But they weren't. They had taken cholera germs with them and soon infected the surrounding countryside.

51

On June 26, an Irish immigrant named Fitzgerald went home from work feeling ill from vomiting, cramps, and diarrhea. Then the Fitzgerald children became ill and died a few days later of an illness the doctor diagnosed as cholera. Although Fitzgerald eventually recovered, his wife caught the disease and died. Forever after, Irish immigrants would be blamed for bringing cholera into the United States.

Sunday, June 29, was observed in New York as a day of fasting and prayer. The next day, Methodists of the city began a series of prayer meetings that would continue for the rest of the summer.

The exodus of citizens continued, and by the end of the first week, almost everyone who could leave New York had gone. As a result, the streets were cleaner, and for the first time in years, the Fourth of July was free of brawls and knifings. As the epidemic continued, the Board of Health issued daily cholera reports. Since few people believed the disease was contagious, citizens gathered on street corners to discuss the latest cases. If cases were reported in widespread parts of the city, how could the victims catch it from one another? Cholera must come from changes in the atmosphere. Concentrations of it in the slum areas were simply due to the shortcomings of the victims or overcrowding, anything that would contribute to contaminating the air.

Most commerce stopped, and as workers lost their jobs, the poor grew poorer and needed more help. So did widows and orphans. Deaths continued to occur, and cartloads of coffins rumbled through the city on their way to the cemeteries.

The immigrants who were crowded into the slums resented any intrusion of authority by city officials, since many had fled their homeland because of unreasonable use of authority there. They wouldn't allow their sick to go to the hospitals and opposed immediate burial of their dead since many had old-world customs that they wanted to follow. Doorways to tenements were blocked by the immigrants to prevent doctors and city officials from coming inside.

The epidemic grew worse. Bodies lay unburied in gutters, and smoke from the burning of bedding and clothing filled the air. People burned tar, pitch, and camphor in hopes of ridding the air of impurities. Houses, stores, and places of worship stood empty, so vandalism and burglaries became common.

Medical treatment followed the usual pattern of bloodletting, blistering, and purging through liberal doses of calomel. Laudanum (a solution whose main ingredient is opium) was also used in great quantities. If those treatments failed, more extreme measures were taken, such as electric shock, tobacco smoke enemas, and injections of saline solutions in the veins.

From these remedies alone, it's easy to understand why many people became afraid to seek medical treatment. A rhyme that grew popular at this time was:

> *Cholera kills and doctors slay,*
> *and every foe will have its way.*[5]

Although physicians could not agree on the treatment of cholera, many agreed on the causes. Marshy lands and atmospheric changes led the list along with filthy living conditions, bad water, and poor diet. But they even disagreed on what a poor diet was!

One of the most outspoken critics of the living habits of Americans at this time was not a doctor at all but an unsuccessful minister who found his true calling as a dietary reformer. Sylvester Graham had been lecturing for several years against the evils of strong drink and tight corsets, and for the good habits of exercise, frequent bathing, fresh air, and a decent diet. Now suddenly, in the midst of the cholera epidemic, his words began to make sense to his listeners.

Graham elaborated, saying that everyone should have "a properly functioning stomach," and told his listeners to achieve this by eating fresh fruits and vegetables as well as wholesome bread containing lots of bran. His words to New York City audiences, whose city officials had banned the sale of "green and unripe fruits of every kind," must have been especially welcome.

He spoke to standing-room-only crowds about his philosophy of health, recommending it as a deterrent to cholera. Some critics nicknamed him "Father Fiber"[6] and laughed at his theories. But the general public had been looking for someone to lead them out of their disease-dominated existence, and they listened. They began to practice and even preach the gospel according to Graham. Eventually, his special kind of Graham bread with its healthful ingredients found its way to tables across the nation. A cracker (now well known as the graham cracker) made according to his dietary recommendations was later manufactured by the Kellogg Company and named for him.

Cholera loosened its grasp on most of the nation as cold weather arrived. The South was spared until the following year when it was hit in epidemic proportions. Then, except for occasional cases, the disease disappeared for fifteen years.

But in 1832, the nation's attention again turned westward as settlers searched for more land and better health. Unfortunately, cholera went along for the ride, traveling west with soldiers on their way to fight the Black Hawk War in northern Illinois. Quickly, the disease moved south via riverboats and stagecoaches, soon arriving at towns and settlements along the Mississippi River.

Large cities were particularly hard hit, but only New Orleans suffered more than New York. One Louisiana doctor said he had drawn enough blood from cholera patients to float the *General Jackson* steamboat.

Those too ill to go on with their westward trek were cared for by the few available doctors in the Midwest, who continued to use the heroic methods of bleed, purge, blister, and vomit. Heroic medicine was considered the normal practice, and the doctor who didn't use it was chastised by his colleagues. But one anonymous physician dared to speak out against it and say the practice was not heroic, it was murderous. Unfortunately, he was right.

THE SPECIALISTS
TAKE OVER

As the midwestern states of Ohio, Indiana, Illinois, and others were being settled, more physicians arrived to practice their art among the settlers. Some were downright quacks; others, merely unskilled. A few were a credit to their profession. Dr. Daniel Drake, in particular, was a man years ahead of his time and fellow practitioners.

His understanding of medicine reached far beyond phlebotomy. Called a "frontiersman of the mind,"[1] he brought medical science to the midwestern frontier and preached common sense during the cholera epidemic. Dr. Drake advised a normal diet, a calm and hopeful mind, and considered quarantine useless against the disease. He believed that filthy cities and people were indirectly to blame for cholera.

A true Renaissance man, Dr. Drake was enthusiastic about learning everything. He wanted to make "physicians of the wilderness, who were isolated and illiterate as he himself once had been, into a medical profession."[2] Soon, he had founded three medical colleges, the first teaching hospital west of the Alleghenies, as well as the first medical society, eye infirmary, circulating library, museum, drugstores, and

A country doctor often traveled miles to see a patient in her rural home, dispensing medicine from his saddlebag. Lack of roads made horseback the only method of transportation in those early days.
(NATIONAL LIBRARY OF MEDICINE)

෴

even the first soda fountain! During this time, he was also teaching at Transylvania Medical College in Kentucky.

Because Dr. Drake was intensely curious, he began to ask other midwestern physicians about geographic conditions in their areas and about the relationship of these conditions to illness and disease. He questioned them about epidemics, trying to find causes and cures. By the early 1830s, he was traveling to gather up information for himself. He firmly believed that the environment had a great influence on health.

Newspapers were not always reliable as a source of information. Editors often reported illness in other communities in order to attract settlers and business investors to their own. The climate was always reported as "salubrious," or healthy, in the newspaper's own town. The October 9, 1838, issue of the Milwaukee, Wisconsin, *Sentinel* reported, "Physicians say that our territory is distressingly healthy."[3] Off the record, however, citizens were angry that Wisconsin had been placed in the sick belt of the nation.

Dr. Drake covered more than 30,000 miles on his fact-finding tours, traveling from the Gulf of Mexico to the Canadian border, and from Pittsburgh, Pennsylvania, to the Rocky Mountains. After nearly twenty years of information gathering, he wrote a book to support his theory. When the *Principal Diseases of the Interior Valley of North America* was finally published in 1850, it was hailed as a medical masterpiece. Eventually, it would lead to a general understanding of causes and cures of disease for that time period and location.

In the frontier society, nothing was ever overlooked as a possible cure for disease or aid to good health. Settlers would try almost anything, even oil or water. Petroleum-based oil had been used by the Seneca Indians before the white man came. When the Senecas found the oil floating on lakes and streams, they dipped their blankets in it and wrung it out into containers for later use. They discovered that rheumatic-type ailments or skin rashes resulting from exposure, insect bites, or disease benefited from oil treatments. During Revolutionary War times, soldiers were allowed to stop on marches and collect the oil to spread on their aching bodies, especially on rheumatic joints. When the soldiers drank the oil, it acted as a laxative.

In the late 1830s, an early entrepreneur named Samuel M. Kier realized the potential in the rapidly expanding health market and sold bottles of "American Oil" as a cure for everything that ailed anybody. (It was the same Seneca Oil used by the Erie Canal builders.) Later, in 1846, Kier published testimonials to the curative powers of his product, stating that it was good for "rheumatism, chronic cough, ague, toothache, corns, neuralgia, piles, urinary disorders, indigestion, and liver ailments."[4] By 1858, he had sold a quarter of a million bottles of oil at one dollar each.

At that same time, another medical specialty, or sect, was gaining in popularity. It was called hydropathy, or hydrotherapy, and its only ingredient was water. Water treatments had been designed by a European, Vincent Priessnitz, after he was involved in a wagon accident that left him with broken bones and a bruised body. Claiming that he was made well by his use of body packs dipped in ice water, Priessnitz promoted his treatment until it was known throughout Europe. When he opened the Water University in his hometown of Grafensberg, in what is now Poland, thousands arrived to take the cure.

By the mid-1800s, Americans also were convinced this latest health craze would cure all their ills. But they needed to be persuaded to immerse their bodies in water, since few Americans yet bathed on a regular basis. Instructions were even printed for reluctant bathers. In Marie Louise Shew's

"Water Cure for Ladies," she explained a step-by-step procedure, stating that "no one need, in the least, fear any remote injurious effect."[5]

The theory of hydrotherapy was simple. Skin reflected a patient's health. If the skin felt dry or looked discolored, that meant disease was trapped inside the body. Watering the outside ensured that the disease could escape. After treatment, if the patient suddenly erupted in boils, acne, or perspiration or suffered a bout of diarrhea, that meant the hydrotherapy was working.

When this idea first reached the United States, even Dr. Benjamin Rush had a word or two to say about it before he died. Recommending baths as a "brace to the animal fibers," he went on to add that the treatment would cure "gout, epilepsy, hysteria, palpitation of the heart, lockjaw, defective hearing, melancholy and madness,"[6] to name only a few problems.

Water-cure establishments, or spas, developed across the country, offering restful stays in beautiful surroundings, with separate "Ladies' Quarters" for women who wanted to find relief from too much childbearing. Following the stringent European methods, the stays could hardly be considered restful, however. Some patients were awakened at three o'clock in the morning, wrapped in cold wet sheets for hours at a time, then plunged into icy water, then given half-baths, then sent off on a three- to four-mile walk, then given another wrap in the dreaded sheets, followed by a sitz and foot bath. Some establishments insisted on thirteen baths a day as well as the consumption of twenty to thirty glasses of water. After many American followers complained, the number of baths was decreased and the temperature of the water was increased.

Water has traditionally had significant spiritual and healing powers, so it's easy to understand the sudden and lengthy popularity of this sect. Water is used in Christian baptisms and Jewish *mikvehs;* it is soothing, cooling, and, as Americans found, it is a cleansing agent as well. Hydrotherapy went on to change the habits of the nation in popularizing swimming, home bathing, and indoor bathrooms.

Today, water therapy is a recognized treatment for controlling fevers, healing burns and inflammation, and in physical therapy. Probably the most popular home remedy is the use of ice packs for swelling or aching joints. Modern water treatments include the use of Jacuzzis, hot tubs, bottled water, and home swimming pools.

Meanwhile, in Europe, medicine was moving beyond water therapy. In the mid-1800s, advances accelerated, driven by breakthroughs in bacteriology. But that had little effect on isolated doctors practicing medicine on the American frontier. Settlers often reverted to the many superstitions that had been handed down to them from their ancestors. If a family member had received the "power" from an elderly relative, he or she was listened to—carefully. Called "granny medicine," the customs and beliefs began even before a baby's birth.

If a birth seemed premature, granny medicine recommended its prevention by drinking the water in which nine eggs had been boiled. If the birth was taking too long, a midwife or relative put snuff on the end of a quill into the pregnant woman's nose. If sneezing brought about the delivery, that child was always known as a quill baby. A baby's birthmarks could be removed by rubbing them with the hand of a corpse. And if the baby should develop croup, it was believed that hiding hair from his head in the hole of an oak tree would prevent whooping cough.

There were superstitions that protected settlers from a

variety of ills: Carrying an onion in a pocket provided protection from snakebite; warts could be given away to two people riding on a gray horse; colds could be treated by eating from a blue dish or drinking stolen milk; and a backache could be cured by turning a somersault at the call of the first whippoorwill of spring.

Hypo (maybe a form of depression) was a serious mental condition characterized by "a lack of desire to attend to any business."[7] However, people did not believe it was a condition of the mind only. It might develop from "hard drink, colds, gout, night air, incessant studying, loss of friends or scolding companions."[8] To cure this condition, doctors recommended phlebotomy, footbaths, and doses of calomel. If people continued to act in a strange manner, the remedy was repeated.

If settlers didn't have their own versions of granny medicine to rely on, books were becoming available for those who wanted to treat themselves. Advice was given for achieving good health, such as: Rise early. Eat simple food. Take plenty of exercise. Recommended exercise for young girls was using a spinning wheel or milking a cow.

The most widely used book in the West was J. C. Gunn's *Domestic Medicine, or Poor Man's Friend.* In A. J. Goodlett's book *Family Physician,* he offered the following advice on amputations: "Any man, unless he is an idiot or an absolute fool, can perform this operation."[9] Since it is doubtful anyone considered himself a fool or an idiot, it's easy to understand why everyone felt capable of performing surgery, as long as someone else was the patient.

As settlers headed farther west, opportunities for anyone and everyone to practice medicine soon expanded along with the frontier.

⤶ 7 ⤷

TRAUMA ON THE TRAIL

Despite diseases and the hardships of travel, the great migration west continued. The motivations for the trip were as varied as the people making it. More land, dreams of wealth, adventure, or better health were only a few.

Major trails across the United States soon developed, following the old ones left by trappers and traders. Those who marched along the antebellum route through what are now the Gulf states had the benefits of warmer climate and better conditions en route.

But they soon learned that disaster and disease could be encountered anywhere. Some groups persuaded physicians to go with them; others had medicine chests containing pills made of opium, camphor, cayenne pepper, and calomel. But most pioneers had no medicines, simply because they were poor or unknowing. Depending on the trail, the destination, and the degree of illness they encountered, the trips lasted anywhere from six to nine months. Boredom and depression were constant companions.

The Santa Fe Trail had been established in 1821, when William Becknell guided an expedition from Independence, Missouri, to Santa Fe, New Mexico. Monthly trips crossed

Alcohol was sometimes the only remedy available for health problems that developed on the frontier; friends or strangers were often the only doctors. (LIBRARY OF CONGRESS)

୶ଚ ଚ୶

that nine-hundred-mile expanse—some of it desert, some of it swamp, but all of it destined to cause discomfort, disability, and disease.

Great stretches along the Arkansas River were inhabited by the *Anopheles* mosquito. Pioneers tried everything to avoid the malaria mosquitoes: smudge pots, netting over exposed skin, and covering themselves with crushed leaves and stems of a plant called pennyroyal, which emits a pungent oil. They even plastered themselves with mud. But they were treating the effect, not the cause, and malaria continued to be a problem, causing one person to remark that it was a "serious opposition to much civilization."[1]

Back in the settled parts of the nation, cinchona bark was used as a treatment for malaria, but the results were discouraging and confusing. Its bulk made it difficult to use in quantity, and it was impossible to give exact dosages. Moreover, when the patient did take it, diarrhea and nausea resulted.

Two French chemists had isolated quinine from cinchona bark in 1822 and found it to be highly effective against malaria. Yet it was not generally known in the United States. Slow to be adopted by American practitioners, quinine would not be used until their heroic methods had been exhausted. By then, their patients were exhausted, too, and, as a result, slow to respond to quinine. In addition, there was confusion over diseases. Doctors labeled other diseases malaria, when in fact they were something else. When quinine was given and the patient failed to respond, quinine was blamed.

Malaria itself could be unpredictable. After being infected by the mosquito, the patient might become ill a few days, a few weeks, or even a few months later. Extremes in temperature, fatigue, high altitude, injury, or heavy exercise factored into the onset and the severity of the disease. Since all these conditions were part of life on the trail, it's understandable why so many pioneers suffered from malaria.

Construction had begun in 1827 on Ft. Leavenworth, located near the junction of the Kansas and Missouri Rivers. Although the site had been chosen at an elevation to avoid the swampy lowlands near the riverbanks where mosquitoes bred, malaria struck anyway, even before the fort was completed. Fortunately for the travelers on the military, civilian, and supply trains who embarked from there, a few doctors, such as John Sappington, understood the benefits of quinine and promoted its cure. Early in his practice, Dr. Sappington had concocted some "Anti-Fever Pills," which were nothing more than quinine disguised in licorice, myrrh, and oil of sassafras. He began to market them in 1832, and they became popular immediately. It was said that bells in frontier towns rang each evening at sunset to remind people to take Dr. Sappington's pills.

During the Mexican War in 1846–47, thousands of soldiers passed through Ft. Leavenworth on their way to battle, carrying guns and quinine to fight two different enemies. When the Mexican War began, the army had only twenty surgeons and fifty assistants to look after one hundred thousand men. The army added a few more to the roster, but it was fortunate that the war produced few casualties. Victory over Mexico gave the United States new territory in what is now California, Nevada, Utah, Arizona, and parts of New Mexico, Colorado, and Wyoming. Now military doctors cared for soldiers in posts even more isolated than before the war. But that was changing as settlers moved westward on more established trails.

The Oregon Trail took shape to the north of the Santa Fe Trail when mountain men first led wagons over its two

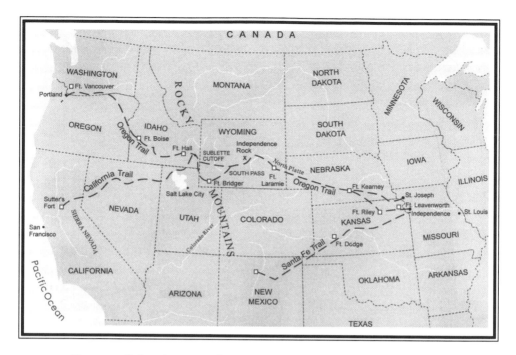

Graves of the pioneers who grew ill and died while heading west
lined the major overland trails to the Pacific Ocean
and the southwest. (AUTHOR)

თ⊚ ⊚ა

thousand miles from Independence, Missouri, to what is now Oregon's Willamette Valley. When a southerly cutoff was established, it became known as the California Trail. Then, in 1847, when members of the Church of Jesus Christ of Latter-day Saints, also known as Mormons, headed west in a mass migration to avoid religious persecution, it also became known as the Mormon Trail.

This well-traveled route was not without the usual hazards of bad weather, contaminated water, poor diet, and uniformed settlers, which all took their toll. It was common practice for wagon trains to camp around a spring, river, or

67

lake. Sometimes the water was clear and pure; often it was murky and polluted. When the pioneers had no choice, they tried to cleanse the bad water by charcoal filtering or using the leaves of prickly pears to settle mud to the bottom of a container. Often the water was so foul-smelling that it could not be tolerated unless coffee was boiled in it. Settlers noted in their diaries that even their horses preferred coffee to water!

Settlers encountered yet another physical problem called scurvy, not knowing in the beginning of the great migration that it was caused by lack of ascorbic acid, or vitamin C, in their diets. Scurvy began to appear after many weeks of a daily diet consisting of little more than salt pork and flapjacks. Sometimes it was mistaken for rheumatism because of the joint aches it caused. Then, when other symptoms such as fatigue, skin sores, and swollen gums appeared, the patient definitely knew what he had. If left untreated, scurvy eventually crippled, maimed, and even killed.

The sad part is that the plants and trees along the trail could have been used as a source of vitamin C to eliminate the suffering and save countless lives. The tips of spruce, fir, or pine trees and wild plants and berries would have easily corrected the diet deficiency. So would ordinary beans, the staple of most American diets at that time. Yet when cholera scares occurred along the trail, beans were thrown away because it was believed they were carriers of the disease!

American pioneers met Mexican people along the Santa Fe trail yet failed to note at first that they were free of scurvy. The reason was their diet. Beans, dried fruits, and pine nuts were staples; red peppers and onions were used for flavor. All contained generous amounts of ascorbic acid.

Trauma, or injuries, on the trail was another health hazard. Animals, both domestic and wild, extreme weather, hostile Indians, guns, and prairie fires caused broken bones, bruises, wounds, and burns, sometimes treatable, sometimes not. Insects such as chiggers, lice, horseflies, and ticks caused such infection and discomfort that settlers sometimes traveled at night to avoid them.

Guns of that day often kicked back with such force that they did more harm to the shooter than to the proposed victim. When a man named Andrew Broadus took aim during a buffalo hunt, he shot himself in the arm instead. Gangrene infection quickly set in, and several days later it became necessary to amputate. He finally persuaded a friend to do it, using the only surgical tools available, a handsaw and a razor. The friend dressed the wound with tar, and it healed completely.

Some of the physicians who traveled west with the wagon trains were spiritual healers as well. Marcus Whitman had traveled to Oregon for the first time in 1835, to use his medical education and religious calling among the Pacific Northwest Indians. However, one of the first persons he treated was Jim Bridger, the famous mountain man, who'd had an arrowhead embedded in his back for three years. Whitman successfully removed the arrow, eleven years before anesthesia was demonstrated in the United States!

Whitman and his wife, Narcissa, worked among the Cayuse and Nez Perce tribes. Both tribes had medicine men called *te-wats*. By tradition, the relatives of the patients were allowed to kill the *te-wats* if their treatment failed.

In 1847, a wagon trail brought an epidemic of measles to the area. Whitman managed to keep the emigrant children alive, but the Indian children had no immunity, and many died. The Cayuse believed that Whitman was responsible, and following their tradition, killed him, his wife, and twelve of his associates.

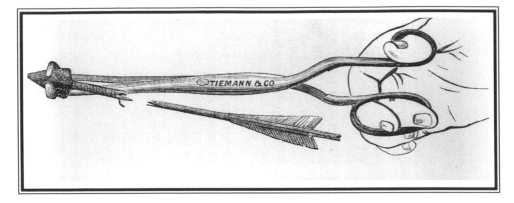

*Special forceps were developed by Army physicians
for the extraction of arrowheads.*
(NATIONAL LIBRARY OF MEDICINE)

Illness and injury continued to plague American settlers on the trail as they pushed back the western frontier. At the same time, pioneers on a worldwide medical frontier were working to find causes and cures for many of those same medical problems confronting Americans. Shortly after the French Revolution in the late 1700s, physicians there had begun a new, exciting period of experimentation. Their findings in bacteriology soon spread, and physicians in Europe started to use biological medicine to prevent disease. Consistent results in European laboratories could not be denied, except in the United States, where skepticism grew and restrictions lessened on the practice of medicine.

In 1838, South Carolina and Maryland removed all legal requirements on medical licenses. New York State followed in 1844, and by 1851, fifteen states did the same. Eight states had never had any legal restrictions at all.

The requirements for entry into medical school were ele-

The EXAMINATION, of a YOUNG SURGEON.

The seriousness of licensing proceedings for a young surgeon was
satirized in an 1811 cartoon by George Cruikshank.
(NATIONAL LIBRARY OF MEDICINE)

mentary at best. Some students applying for admission were illiterate. When they left school, most doctors could not or would not keep up with medical advances and only pursued the wealthiest patients. Five different doctors usually had five different opinions, and they produced few good results. Failures were the rule, and only surgeons managed to be respected because there was but one way to set a leg or remove a bullet. The profession of medicine in the United States was declining into a period of confusion.

✎ 8 ✐

THE ART OF HEALING

Two physicians practiced among San Francisco's eight hundred citizens the day that news of James Marshall's discovery reached the city. A few weeks earlier, on January 24, 1848, Marshall had found sizable gold nuggets in the mill race, a ditch that channeled water from the river to the mill near Sutter's Fort, where he worked. Gradually, the news leaked out to California and then to the rest of the nation. Drs. Victor Jean Fourgeaud and John Townsend hoped to strike it rich in the Sierra foothills. But they didn't really desert their patients; they all left together! By June, more than 80 percent of San Francisco's population had left town. So, even if the doctors had stayed, business would certainly have been slow.

In December, President James K. Polk announced the gold strike was genuine, and the big rush was on. Because much of the nation was gripped by harsh winter weather, the overland trails were closed until spring. Therefore, most of the first gold seekers chose one of two ocean routes. The passengers were called argonauts in honor of the mythological heroes who traveled by ship in search of treasure.

The longer route was an eighteen-thousand-mile voyage

around South America via Cape Horn. Although this passage could last anywhere from four to eight months, it was far easier, physically, than any other route. Generally, fresh fruits, vegetables, and water were available part of the time, obtained at ports of call along the way, and weather was warm and balmy for some of the trip. Although living conditions were crowded and unsanitary, and some of the passengers suffered from scurvy, most people survived the trip.

The fastest, but more hazardous, water/land route to the gold fields lay across the Isthmus of Panama. The six- to eight-week trip probably seemed longer as passengers first sailed to Panama City, which was little more than a collection of infested mud huts on the Atlantic Ocean side of the Isthmus. From there, gold seekers hiked, climbed, rode mules, and floated the remaining miles to Chagres, another infested mud-hut village on the Pacific Ocean side of the Isthmus. Although hotels advertised their availability along the route, they consisted primarily of such crude shelters as rafts turned upside down on four poles, or a small tent "containing three cots, one table, and two plates."[1]

Drenching rain and torrid heat turned Panama into a miserable breeding ground for one health problem after another, with one significant exception. Although cholera had come back to the United States in 1848, brought by European immigrants who jumped quarantine in New York Harbor, the earliest argonauts had apparently escaped it in their mad dash for gold. They left the East before they became infected.

The nation seemed resigned to another epidemic, and most everyone agreed with the journalist who wrote in the *Milwaukee Weekly Wisconsin* on December 27, 1848, that "another spring will bring the cholera among us sweeping like the Angel of Death over our firesides." And he was right. With the spring of 1849, another epidemic began.

Things hadn't changed much in public or civic response to the filthy surroundings that nurtured infestation. Pigs still roamed the streets of major cities, acting as street sweepers, with a new wrinkle added to the general confusion: Pignapping became common as men gathered up unwatched pigs to sell to butchers. Maybe it was just as well: Pigs had begun to fight with the citizens for space on the streets and even attacked small children.

Most California-bound pioneers chose to ignore the threat of cholera and went ahead with their plans, believing there was little they could do against the disease anyway. Although new work in biology led to theories that cholera might be caused by microscopic organisms, no one yet understood this except the doctors. In fact, not all of *them* understood it either, some even agreeing with the general public that the atmosphere around them or the ground beneath them was somehow responsible for the disease.

From Independence and St. Joseph, Missouri, wagon trains hurried west in such great numbers during the Gold Rush that the narrow, two-furrowed tracks became miles-wide trails, with prairie grasses trampled and eaten until there was little left for the oxen and horses that would follow. Soon the trails also became lined with graves, with only the victims' names and the word *cholera* chiseled onto small wooden crosses. The disease ravaged the overland pioneers, sometimes taking half of an entire party. As one observer noted, "Many have left their bones to bleach on the great plains of Nebraska."[2]

Indians were gold seekers, too, and often suffered the same fate. One traveler noted Sioux lodges in the valley of the Platte River but saw no sign of life. When he investigated, he found the entire encampment dead, apparently from cholera.

An epidemic belt seemed to extend a distance of six to seven hundred miles west from the Missouri towns where the trains began. Just beyond Fort Laramie, near the North Platte River in what is now Wyoming, cholera disappeared due to this region's higher altitudes and cooler weather. But other diseases were waiting to take its place.

As the pioneers approached the Rocky Mountains, spotted fever, carried by ticks, began to plague them with high fevers, aching bones and muscles, and painful headaches. Mumps, measles, and even insanity also carried off victims. One woman, however, claimed to be actually *cured* of something, insisting that her epilepsy had gone away during the journey. It can also be noted that cases of obesity and hypochondria also disappeared on the trail.

Starvation and exposure to the harsh climate of desert and mountains were the final scourges that pioneers endured before reaching California. With a little careful planning, these problems might have been avoided, but planning was not a consideration in the rush for gold.

Argonauts arriving by sea turned San Francisco into an unwieldy gathering place of nearly forty thousand by the end of 1850. Its climate was damp, its living accommodations filthy, and people grew ill from conditions they encountered in California or from the diseases they brought with them. Although there were 626 physicians in the city by the end of that same year, and a hospital opened, fees were high and equipment and care were poor. People had little interest in anyone else's health as long as they themselves remained healthy. They were only interested in gold.

Pioneers arriving via the overland routes set up makeshift accommodations around Sutter's Fort, thereby estab-

*Working conditions during the California Gold Rush were not
kind to the miners who endured physical hardships that
often led to serious illness.*
(STATE OF CALIFORNIA, DIVISION OF BEACHES AND PARKS)

lishing Sacramento, the future capital of the state. Because
of swampy ground, and the fact that too many people arrived
before their basic needs of food and shelter could be met,
settlers began dying at the rate of twenty per day. This could
have wiped out the entire community within a few months
if the new arrivals had not been coming in such numbers as
to double the population in that same time.

Cholera didn't break out in California until 1850, arriving by sea. When the steamer *Carolina* docked on October 7 at San Francisco, many on board were infected but were not quarantined to the ship. The disease quickly spread to the city and then to Sacramento. By the end of November, 364 of that city's 6,000 residents had died. Apparently, not many people had followed one doctor's advice to avoid cholera: Cover up in bed with hot bricks and ears of boiled corn. Then again, maybe they had.

Doctors were susceptible to gold fever, too, and before the rush ended a few years later, more than 1,500 would be at work in the hills and cities, either as medical practitioners or as miners. No laws, examinations, or regulations applied to the practice of medicine in the early days of the Gold Rush, simply because there was no state government to write or enforce them. California did not become a state until the autumn of 1850. Any man could hang up a sign and call himself a doctor.

Never had the status of the American medical profession sunk so low in the eyes of the population. Once regarded as dignified and noble, doctors were now thought of as unethical quacks. They became the targets of the press and the public. To quote a common saying: Cholera may come now and then, but doctors are always with us.

This was not the first time that white man's medicine had been practiced in California territory. Eurocentric methods of healing were introduced by the Spanish when they first explored Mexico in the 1500s, and they established the first hospital in the Western Hemisphere there in 1503. When the Spanish traveled north in the 1700s to claim territory for the Crown in Alta California, medical care for whites and Indians was provided by the Franciscan fathers at their missions. Father Junipero Serra was particularly interested in the effects of citrus fruits on scurvy and urged the planting of these trees at each mission he founded.

Gold Rush doctors in the towns and mining camps found familiar diseases they'd treated back east, with one basic difference: The patients waited too long to find help. Because of the distant places and terrible conditions in which they lived, they were in a far weaker state when they finally sought medical attention. One out of five miners died in the first year. That those other four survived is more than surprising; it's a miracle.

A shortage of decent food developed early in the rush as farmers had left their crops to rot in the fields while they raced off to the mines. No one was available to plant new crops to replace the ruined ones. It's not surprising, then, that scurvy continued to plague the miners, and some interesting self-cures developed as a result. Burying the patient in the ground with only his head protruding was one of the strangest cure attempts on record. In fact, a traveler found an entire mining camp buried up to their necks, with only a few healthy miners above ground to stand guard against attack by marauding animals.

The best and the worst medicine was practiced during the Gold Rush. The James King case illustrates this point. King was shot late one afternoon by an angry citizen for attacks made on him in King's San Francisco newspaper, the *Daily Evening Bulletin*. As King staggered into the Pacific Express office, bleeding profusely, two doctors rushed to his side. They were well-educated in the traditional sense but disagreed on what to do for the patient. A third doctor arrived, then a fourth, then a fifth. Finally, there were twenty doctors in attendance, each probing the wound, arguing about a course of treatment, and puffing on cigars until the air became thick with smoke. When night arrived and nothing had yet been done, the patient was placed on a counter, and the physicians took turns keeping vigil.

Meanwhile, an angry crowd had gathered outside the jail where the gunman had taken refuge. The crowd organized itself into the Second Committee of Vigilance and called on the governor, demanding an immediate trial and execution.

Perhaps the confrontation might have ended there if King had recovered. But he died three days later, still without any medical intervention. Later, during an autopsy, it was discovered that the wound was a ruptured vein and the patient would probably have recovered with proper treatment.

The Committee of Vigilance carried out its own brand of justice, hanging the man who shot King at the very moment of King's funeral. In 1857, the attending physicians were called before the State Medical Convention to decide if there actually had been a murder, or if death was caused by badly handled treatment of a minor injury. Finally, after much public debate in both the newspapers and on the street, the doctors were cleared in the courts. But in the minds of citizens of that day, they had practiced bad medicine.

As a French physician noted, "In this land of gold, no law governs the art of healing."[3]

৩ 9 ৩

DOCTORS WANTED: NO
WOMEN NEED APPLY

I t's been said that every nineteenth-century woman doctor was a pioneer, struggling to open the medical frontier to her presence. Although women had been healers for centuries, they worked particularly hard in this nation to become recognized physicians. In ancient Greece and Egypt, and also during the Middle Ages, women had been easily accepted as midwives, people trained to help in childbirth. There was disapproval, however, if females tried to study the same curriculum as men and become physicians. Only in Italy did women have access to identical medical training. Women in Roman times usually specialized as doctors of obstetrics and gynecology, although one woman doctor named Antiochis was credited with the discovery of a medicine for rheumatism and sciatica.[1]

In American colonial times, many women had large practices as midwives and some even practiced a family-type medicine, but women were barred from attending medical schools or becoming apprenticed to physicians. In the early eighteenth century, as the services of more apprentice-trained men became available, women were forced from family practice.

Martha Ballard, who lived in Maine during the mid-eighteenth century, may have been typical of midwives of colonial days. In her diary, she recorded delivering her first baby—as a midwife—in July 1778. Before this, she probably assisted at many other births because this was the age of "social childbirth,"[2] when female relatives and neighbors came together to attend a birth and assist, if need be. Since Mrs. Ballard already had nine of her own children by 1778, she had much experience with the birth process.

Her expertise didn't end here. Like other midwives of her day, she applied poultices, dressed burns, treated dysentery and diseases such as scarlet fever (which was then called canker rash). She also lanced abscesses, reduced swelling, and induced vomiting, but seldom practiced phlebotomy. Most midwives, including Mrs. Ballard, left bleeding to the "regular," or academic, doctors.

Mrs. Ballard was an herbalist and made pills, salves, and ointments from the herbs she grew in her garden or picked along country lanes. In her diary, published as *A Midwife's Tale*, she mentions giving dock root "for the itch,"[3] applying a poultice of basswood "to Manlys foot it being sweld,"[4] and using saffron, commonly prescribed for infants. To one child ill with a "soar mouth,"[5] she gave honey and saffron.

Mrs. Ballard also bought from a doctor certain drugs and herbs which she then mixed and prescribed herself. Since nearly all "regular" doctors were herbalists, too, they were in direct competition with midwives in this part of their practices. However, it mattered little to the men who were the "regulars" as long as the midwives were not called doctors and continued to be barred from their schools and teacher-student training.

Mrs. Ballard was devoted to her patients, crossing frozen rivers, forging streams, and sitting up many nights, sometimes risking her own health. She continued to deliver babies and treat illnesses until she died at the age of seventy-seven in 1812. She was well-known and liked, and highly regarded as a midwife in her community. Yet all official records and property were in her husband's name, despite the fact that her earnings paid for much of it. Had it not been for her diary, which was not written for publication, there would have been no trace of this remarkable woman's life. Even her grave was unmarked.

When medical schools began to flourish after the War of 1812 ended, they continued to be for men only. Women were forced to be content with their roles as midwives. By the middle of the 1800s, the profession of medicine was rapidly disintegrating. It was a time ready-made for women to step in.

Medical theory and practice were in a state of transition. The old heroic methods of bleed, purge, blister, and vomit were being questioned by the public. The use of anesthesia was new, and it challenged the older idea that the patient must suffer and feel pain to get well.

Dr. Crawford W. Long of Georgia is credited with being the first doctor to give ether as an anesthesia. As a medical student he had attended "ether frolics," where students inhaled ether to intoxication. Remembering this experience, he used ether as an anesthetic in 1842. It remained little known until some time later, when a dentist, Dr. William Morton of Boston, gave it to a patient before extracting an ulcerated tooth. From there, it developed into general use in surgical practices. Chloroform was discovered in 1851 by a British surgeon, and surgeons soon preferred it since it was less dangerous to the patient.

Anti-elitism continued to flourish during this period in American history, and worked against the medical profession. "Every man his own physician"[6] was a slogan that was widely followed. Since women had long been considered the moral housekeepers of the family, it seemed time for women to step in and clean house morally in the medical profession.

Even more significant, women's overall role in society was changing. Industrialization had altered both work and family lifestyles. Many men were going to work in factories and large shops, away from the sphere of the family-owned farms and cottage industries. Suddenly, women became more powerful at home, and their authority within the family became more acceptable. Slowly, their influence began to be felt in the social and public sectors of American life.

For many years, Elizabeth Blackwell had been a teacher, one of the few professions open to women in the early nineteenth century. She had conducted a private school with her mother and sister, but she longed to become a physician. Finally, with enough money saved from her teaching career to support a new life, she applied to many medical schools.

After months of rejection, she finally was accepted by Geneva Medical School in upstate New York, in October 1847. But even that was an accident. Not wanting to be the one to turn down an application by a woman, the president of the school asked the all-male student body if they would agree to a female student in their midst. Thinking it was a joke, the students voted the opposite of how they felt. They voted to accept her.

Blackwell moved to Geneva, ignoring the jeers of the townspeople as she walked through the streets from school to boardinghouse. Although she was excluded from classroom demonstrations on medical subjects, she persevered, graduating in 1849 at the top of her class. Later that year, she sailed to Europe for further studies.

When news of Blackwell's acceptance reached forty-two-

Elizabeth Blackwell (1821–1910) first studied anatomy and
medicine from books while supporting herself as a teacher.
(NEW YORK PUBLIC LIBRARY)

year-old Harriet Hunt, she immediately applied to Harvard
Medical School. Hunt had been a practitioner of self-help
medicine for twelve years, but still she was rejected. She did
receive permission to buy tickets to the medical lectures at
the school, however, but was reminded that this did not
mean she would be entitled to a degree.

In 1851, the Harvard Medical School's senior class presented a resolution to the faculty to protest the admission of women. Harvard's trustees passed this resolution, and it remained in effect until 1946!

Influenced by Elizabeth Blackwell's success, Ann Preston read with a mentor for two years and then applied to medical schools. She received one rejection after another. A group of Quaker male physicians heard of her experience and decided to help her and other women who wanted a medical education. In 1850, these physicians founded the Women's Medical College of Pennsylvania with a student body of forty. Located in Philadelphia, it was the nation's first medical school for "doctoring ladies."[7] At commencement ceremonies fourteen months later, fifty policemen stood guard against a threatened invasion by male medical students who wanted to stop the proceedings. But nothing came of the threat.

Male physicians refused to accept women in their professional midst because they didn't want the competition in an already crowded and unpopular profession. There were other reasons as well. They considered it improper for women to examine men during physicals or to discuss anything about their condition that could be considered sexual. Medical societies rejected women as members, and male doctors would not consult with them. If a male physician dared to hold a professional consultation with a female doctor, he was shunned by other male doctors.

Rumors spread that women doctors had inferior intellects, physical weaknesses, and tendency toward hysteria which rendered them unstable and undependable. Later, a Harvard professor named E. H. Clarke wrote a book called *Sex in Education,* in which he said that higher education in women produced "monstrous brains and puny bodies," and "flowing thoughts and constipated bowels."[8]

Opinions in this book were soon challenged by medical women, in particular Dr. Mary Putnam Jacobi. With careful analysis and case studies, she proved that women's health was able to withstand the rigors of performing medical duties. Dr. Jacobi became a strong role model for all the young women of the time who were thinking of entering the field: she was able to maintain a large practice, marry, and have a family.

On May 1, 1857, the New York Infirmary for Women and Children opened. This institution guaranteed women students practical experience to add to academic studies, which would complete a well-rounded education. Other women's medical schools opened in Boston, Cleveland, and Baltimore. Since they had little competition, these colleges set higher standards for entrance exams and graduation. As a result, reforms were forced on men's medical schools. Professors were put on salary instead of charging lecture fees to make a living, and students had to spend more time in school and pass all of their exams to graduate.

In 1858, the Women's Medical College was ostracized, which made it impossible for women to attend public teaching clinics in Philadelphia or become members in local medical societies, including the American Medical Association. (Women were not given full membership in that organization until 1915.) Dr. Ann Preston decided that the Women's Medical College would establish its own teaching clinics. Not until after the Civil War would women win the right to attend lectures and clinics at all men's medical colleges. Even then they would be met with jeers, groaning, and stamping of feet as they entered lecture halls. Some women were actually stoned by male students as they left.

Between 1820 and 1870, death rates increased in large cities as more immigrants came to the United States and slum conditions developed as a result of overcrowding. Smallpox and malaria were now preventable, yet deaths from them still occurred among the poor and the uninformed. Statistics would show that death rates were highest among children of the poor.

Industrialization had altered not only men's and women's lifestyles but also the lives of children. When cotton mills opened in the New England states, a demand for child labor resulted. By 1831, half of the employees were children between the ages of seven and twelve. Finally, in 1842, Massachusetts passed a child-labor law stipulating that no child under fourteen years of age could work more than ten hours per day. By then, however, the ill effects of bad housing and long work hours had led to many deaths among the young. Overworked, worn-out children simply could not avoid the infectious diseases that sped through the workplace, and their crowded slum homes and poor diets were not conducive to recovery.

Dr. Elizabeth Blackwell and her younger sister, Dr. Emily Blackwell, called all women physicians the "connecting link"[9] between the medical profession and the everyday life of women because of their concern about family and preventive medicine. Dr. Harriet Hunt added her voice, saying that the female physician must now "prevent as well as cure."[10]

The New York Infirmary established the position of "sanitary visitor" so that young interns could go into the slum areas of cities to teach cleanliness, ventilation, nutrition, and family hygiene. Soon other hospitals followed suit. In 1868, the New York Infirmary became the first hospital in the country to appoint a professor to teach preventive medicine.

Women doctors continued their pioneering efforts, particularly in the care of women and children. Women had long been susceptible to puerperal fever, or childbed fever—an infection that began during childbirth. Hungarian physician Dr. Ignaz Semmelweis noted that women died after childbirth more often when male doctors examined them than when female midwives did. He soon found the reason for this.

Not realizing there was a connection between contagion and surgery or childbirth, male physicians moved from performing autopsies to examining women before, during, or after childbirth, without washing their hands. Midwives, however, only delivered babies. They were not even allowed to attend autopsies. Semmelweis set up a system so that before a woman in labor was examined, everyone washed with soap and water, then dipped their hands in a chlorinated lime solution. Deaths from puerperal fever decreased dramatically.

In 1851, Semmelweis was credited with being the first to bring asepsis (the procedure for keeping germs away from patients) to the attention of the medical world. Since women physicians in this country were already advocating sanitation and hygiene for patients in hospitals, they may have been putting Semmelweis's theory into practice even as his findings were being published.

During the Civil War, women played an important part in upgrading care in military hospitals and on the battlefield. Women's relief societies stepped in to promote better sanitary care, more healthful food, and fresh air. At first, nursing was done by convalescent soldiers. Then Dorothea Dix became the first superintendent of army nurses for the Union army, and women were allowed in the hospitals to care for convalescent men. Dix decreed that the nurses be strong, middle-aged, and plain. She wanted no wartime romances to blossom.

When the war first began, Clara Barton advertised in her hometown newspaper, the *Worcester* (Massachusetts) *Spy,* for provisions for the wounded. Readers responded quickly, donating food and medical supplies. Although she had no official position, she went through battle lines to bring provisions to the soldiers. During the first four years after the war, she was in charge of the search for missing men. She went on to become the founder of the American Red Cross.

Women physicians also served in the war, and the most well-known was Dr. Mary Walker, who graduated from Syracuse Medical College in June 1855, the only female in her class. Perhaps as famous for her manner of dress as for her presence on the battlefield, her tunic and bloomer uniform created more than a little interest among both Rebel and Federal soldiers. In 1864, she received the Congressional Medal of Honor for her heroic work in the war. It was later declared unwarranted and revoked, but she refused to return it and wore it proudly until she died at the age of eighty-six.

Women returned from the battlefield with renewed dedication to the art of healing. Gradually, they became accepted into, or tolerated by, the medical mainstream. In 1864, Dr. Rebecca Lee became the first black woman to receive a medical degree. Soon many of the existing schools became coeducational, and some of the women's schools merged with the men's. At first, however, women students had to sit behind screens during lectures or attend separate classes, and they could examine male patients above the neck only. By 1941, only six out of seventy-seven medical schools would still be closed to women.

In 1860, there were fewer than 200 women physicians. In the 1880s, there were 2,400. One of them was Dr. Mary

Hobart, who, in 1884, graduated from the Women's Medical College of the New York Infirmary, founded by Dr. Elizabeth Blackwell. That same year, Dr. Hobart inherited her great-great-grandmother Martha Ballard's diary, which became *A Midwife's Tale*. And in the same year, the Massachusetts Medical Society voted to accept women as members after a debate that had gone on for more than thirty years.

Dr. Hobart became a member of the state society, then applied for membership into the society in the district where she would practice. Before she could be admitted, the examiner wrote for more instructions on acceptable credentials, saying that "there are no women's colleges on the authorized list."[11]

It was a good beginning, but women's pioneering in the world of medicine was far from over.

～❧ 10 ❧～

WHEN BEANS KILLED
MORE MEN THAN
BULLETS

When the American Civil War ended and historians began to figure its cost and weigh its value, they decreed it had been the most important military event in a century. It certainly didn't start out that way in April 1861. No one thought it would last longer than ninety days, and no one took it seriously. As troops from the North and the South moved together for the first big battle in July, people began calling it a *picture-book war* because it was expected to be short and uncomplicated. Many made plans to attend the battle.

But neither side was prepared. The Union army's fifteen thousand men were scattered across the country, poorly equipped, and untrained. Medically speaking, it was in even worse shape. Although the army had started to use ambulances in 1859, they had not been well maintained. Medical supplies were few or nonexistent. Medical officers lacked sufficient understanding of camp sanitation, preventive medicine, and proper hygiene when great numbers of men are temporarily housed and fed in unsanitary conditions.

The Confederacy had just been formed, and its army was smaller in size and numbers, although superior to the

North's in its saber-rattling enthusiasm for the cause. Determined to decide on the slavery issue themselves, eleven states had seceded from the Union in order to preserve slavery and states' rights.

Slavery had once been common in all states. Although it was gone in the North by 1800, it had become a permanent institution in the South.

Africans brought with them some of their own medical beliefs in natural remedies, as well as warm-climate diseases such as dengue. Although there were doctors among them, once the Africans arrived in America, their health became the responsibility of their masters. The owners had control not only over health issues but over living and working conditions as well.

Owners tried to justify the slave system with claims that blacks had immunity to certain diseases, which whites lacked, so slaves could be sent into disease-ridden rice fields and canebrakes without endangering their health. At first, it was thought that most blacks were immune to malaria and yellow fever, but no one knew for sure. It may have been that they had previously contracted these diseases in Africa or had milder attacks that were not recognized.

But for many Africans, immunity came only after repeated attacks of certain diseases. When blacks moved or were sold to owners in other parts of the country, they often had various malarial-type episodes from different parasites and had to endure a period of seasoning.

Serious respiratory problems developed among the blacks simply because they were not used to the colder climate. In addition, inadequate housing, clothing, and diet gave them little means to fight off colds, influenza, pleurisy, and pneumonia. They lived in quarters so small that disease was easily transmitted through the entire row of cramped houses with little ventilation, damp earthen floors, and no sanitation facilities.

Slaves also contended with intestinal diseases, which they contracted when working outside in warm weather. Shoes became important in disease prevention to protect them from insects and larvae that lived in the ground. Accidents also took their lives or left them gravely injured. Farm machines, animals, cuts from axes and scythes, and whippings dealt harsh wounds that sometimes permanently crippled the victim.

When blacks became ill, their status as slaves complicated the recovery process. The slave was required to tell his master if he was ill; then he was entitled to time off from work. But the slave was reluctant to report illnesses because of the harsh methods of treatment to which he would be subjected. He preferred his own self-help remedies or an herb and root doctor. Then, because white owners did not trust black medicine, he had to hide his illness and continue working. Either way, the slave suffered.

If the slave elected to tell about his illness, the owner, his wife, or overseer attempted treatment at first, often using the Thomsonian botanic medicines to heal. The larger plantation owners had set aside a building for a hospital and nursery where one person could care for all the sick. But illness spread rapidly here.

If home remedies didn't work, a physician was called. Some of the owners had humanitarian concerns for their slaves and a real desire to restore them to good health. Nearly all owners had economic reasons for wanting the slaves to be well. They were considered viable only if they survived for five years, and few of the first generation did. The second generation of slaves had longer life expectancies and then were thought to be a financially practical asset.

As the blacks adapted to this country, they devised more home remedies of their own, based on local herbs and roots. Eventually, successful remedies were handed down through several generations. Even the white owners adapted the beneficial ones, such as milkweed, which was used by blacks in Virginia to replace quinine for malaria. James Pawpaw, a Virginia slave, developed a cure for yaws, a tropical infectious disease, through the use of mercury. He received his freedom and an annual pension for the discovery.

Black women acted as prenatal and obstetrical nurses for both black and white women, also practicing midwifery with great success. Physicians saw obstetrical cases only when there was a serious complication.

By 1861, white owners were responsible for the health of four million black slaves, many of whom would go with their white masters while they served in the Confederate army. Other blacks would escape north to serve as soldiers, not servants, in the Union army.

Now both sides felt ready to start the war. July 21, 1861, was a hot and humid Sunday. Thirty thousand Union troops marched twenty-seven miles in scorching heat toward Manassas Junction, Virginia, to meet twenty-two thousand Confederates for the first Battle of Bull Run. Most had gone without breakfast and many without supper the night before. However, the hundreds of northern civilians who had ridden out in their fine carriages to watch the battle had packed picnic lunches and carried opera glasses. They were prepared, even if the soldiers were not.

When the battle began, it seemed that the Union army would win the conflict. But that perception was short-lived. Suddenly, the Federals were in full-blown retreat, fleeing back to Washington without any organization or anyone in authority. Chaos resulted.

In their hasty retreat, ambulance drivers had left the wounded stranded on the battlefield. In fact, not a single wounded Union soldier reached safety in an ambulance. One soldier, whose arm had been amputated, walked the twenty-seven miles back to Washington to an improvised hospital. Many others in even worse condition did the same.

In the city, soldiers collapsed on lawns and sidewalks along Pennsylvania Avenue as nurses circulated among them, handing out coffee and tending their wounds. For President Abraham Lincoln, looking down from the White House, it was a heart-wrenching sight. Together, both sides lost 4,500 wounded, dead, or missing men on this one frightening afternoon.

A Sanitary Commission, made up of civilians, had been appointed by President Lincoln in June to oversee the promotion of the health and welfare of the Union army. Now they began to argue for better equipment, especially ambulances, better food, decent field hospitals, and medicine. Newly appointed Surgeon General William A. Hammond began to push through much-needed reforms, often making political enemies both in Congress and in the army.

In the South, Dr. Samuel Preston Moore was appointed to the same position in July, ruffling no political egos during his four years in office. However, he lacked a transportation system and had fewer medical supplies and well-trained doctors to assist him. Hospitals were also rare. It was said that in the South, every house was considered a hospital.

Meanwhile, the second Battle of Bull Run began on August 29, 1862, and it turned out to be another disaster for the North. Southern Generals Robert E. Lee and Thomas J. (Stonewall) Jackson outmaneuvered the Union troops and overran the field where the wounded lay. Union generals arranged a truce to care for the wounded, but three days after the encounter, three thousand men still lay where they had fallen. Some remained there for six or seven days.

The handling of the injured was slowed down by civilian teamsters hired by the Quartermaster Corps to drive the ambulances. Many of the drivers ran away during the conflict, so instead of having 170 ambulances at hand, they had forty-five. In Washington, the army commandeered trucks, hacks, wagons, anything with wheels, and volunteers drove them. But many of them, too, turned cowardly and ran.

One of Hammond's reforms demanded that the army form an Ambulance Corps and that it be governed by the Medical Corps rather than the quartermasters. It was not until 1864 that an Ambulance Corps Act was finally passed, giving the Medical Corps the right to choose and examine the men assigned to it.

Contagious diseases were another major force to contend with in military campaigns during the war. Diseases were unpredictable and uncontrollable, causing more deaths than bullets. In the battle for Vicksburg, Mississippi, an epidemic of malaria made it impossible for the Union army to attack from the rear. There had been little medical planning and preparation for this campaign, and supplies of quinine were quickly exhausted. A stalemate existed at Vicksburg until General Ulysses S. Grant received more supplies and healthier soldiers.

Many of the new recruits on both sides were pioneers from remote areas who had not been exposed to the contagious diseases running rampant over the rest of the nation. Once they arrived at camp, however, they soon developed measles, chicken pox, scarlet fever, mumps, and other childhood illnesses to which they had never been exposed.

In addition, because of the complete lack of sanitation, insects were everywhere, acting as carriers of contagious fevers. Malaria, typhoid and yellow fevers, diphtheria, diarrhea, and dysentery roared indiscriminately through both Confederate and Union camps. Even the horses got sick from their contagious equine disease, glanders. So little was done about camp cleanliness in the beginning that it was said an encampment could be smelled for miles.

Diet was another problem. At first, Union soldiers were issued an amount of salt pork, bread, and one vegetable a day, usually beans. Later, the government augmented that with three pounds of potatoes a week, then declaring the Union soldiers the best fed in the world. But both sides went hungry on many occasions. When soldiers drove deep into enemy territory, supply lines couldn't reach them, so they lived off the land or just didn't eat.

If food did arrive, it was usually spoiled because there was no refrigeration. The meat was salted so much to prevent spoilage that it had to be soaked in water before it could be cooked. Then it usually became tainted from the cooking water. One soldier said the meat came in two colors, the outside being "as black as a shoe, the inside yellow with putrefaction."[1] Loaves of bread were so spoiled that they were called "worm castles"[2] by the soldiers, and new recruits were told to eat the bread in the dark so they couldn't see what they were eating.

As bad as the food was, cooking made it worse. Food handled by men who didn't wash themselves or the pans they used only further contaminated it. "Beans killed more [men] than bullets,"[3] an officer remarked late in the war. Soldiers cooked for themselves until 1863, when Congress passed an act requiring trained personnel to do this job.

The Union army was better prepared when, on September 17, 1862, it entered the Battle of Antietam near Sharpsburg, Maryland. Seventy-one field hospitals had been set up, mostly in barns and houses, and evacuation of the wounded was carefully planned. While ambulances operated on a regular schedule, many of the injured walked twenty miles back to Frederick, Maryland, stopping halfway at Middletown for food, drink, and medical attention. At Frederick, they were put on straw in railroad freight cars for the trip to hospitals in Washington, Philadelphia, or Baltimore.

Field hospitals now began to follow a certain routine. When the patient was brought in, he was ignored if mortally or slightly wounded. The one who looked as if he could be saved with surgery was taken to an examining table, which was usually a door yanked off a house or barn. The examination was performed even as the patient could see the piles of arms, legs, and corpses lying all around him. Chloroform was the anesthesia of choice rather than ether, since it was less bulky and not flammable. When the patient was unconscious, the surgeon wiped his knife on an already bloody apron, and the cutting began.

Chances for the patient were better if he suffered a wound in an arm or leg because they could easily be amputated. About sixty thousand amputations were performed in the war, and three-quarters of the patients survived. Amputees were generally happy to be alive and proud to have served the nation, on either side. One young veteran said, "I have not lost an arm, I gave it to my country."[4] Many continued to serve throughout the war. The Union had an Invalid Corps of clerks, cooks, and watchmen. The Confederates used amputees to guard hospitals and depots.

Wounds to the torso were almost always fatal; a surgeon simply couldn't reach those penetrating wounds. Abdominal wounds had a mortality rate of 87 percent. (Only 3 percent of Americans failed to survive similar injuries in World War II.) Wounds caused by musket or rifle balls made of lead did more damage than their steel counterparts of today. Infection did the rest. Total Union deaths were approximately 200,000 from disease and 110,000 from combat. Confederates lost 60,000 to disease and 74,000 to combat.

Medical historians have said that the Civil War took place at the close of the medical middle ages, just before bacteriology was understood and aseptic surgery became possible in this country. But Louis Pasteur's work in bacterial origins had been going on in France for years, and others in Europe were researching asepsis. Why not here?

The basic difference between American and European scientists was in their understanding and acceptance of the origin of infection itself. American doctors believed that infections came from filth through the air, and that there was no way to halt the spread of infection until it invaded the patient's wound. Only then did the doctor feel he could do something about it. He poured carbolic acid or bromine into the wound to halt the infection, but not over his hands or instruments.

Some applications were discovered during the Civil War period, then forgotten, only to be rediscovered at a later time. Doctors had tried to keep maggots out of injuries but found that they actually cleaned out dead tissue and prevented gangrene. This phenomenon had been discovered during the Napoleonic Wars in Europe, now again during the Civil War, and would be rediscovered during World War I in 1914–18.

From the first to the last battle of the Civil War, the Medical Department of the United States grew from total chaos to a well-ordered system. A trained hospital corps had emerged from the inept stretchermen and cowardly ambulance drivers. Field hospitals had become organized and well equipped to cut casualties on the battlefields. Tent hospitals

THE SURGEON AT WORK AT THE REAR DURING AN ENGAGEMENT.—[SEE PAGE 635.]

Many physicians who later practiced medicine on the Western
frontier had first received hands-on experience while
serving on Civil War battlefields.
(*LIBRARY OF CONGRESS*)

ఆ⊚ గ్ఞ

at Antietam taught an important lesson of wartime medicine
that carried over into peacetime. Surgical cases treated out
of doors or in well-ventilated housing showed lower mortality and shorter recovery times than those treated in over-
crowded, stifling rooms. Understanding of the causes of
contagion took giant strides from this one fact alone.

There had also been a modest improvement in surgical
technique during the war. The greatest improvement, however, came in terms of experience. The war served as a post-

graduate course for physicians in training. By the time they returned to civilian life, they had seen more types of illness and more kinds of injury than they ever dreamed possible. Many of them headed back to the frontier, ready for anything.

It was the Confederate and Union soldiers, however, who probably learned more about health than anyone else. From camp experience alone, they had discovered that personal and public cleanliness made a direct contribution to their individual health. As they returned to their homes in settled areas or on the frontier, they would soon begin to look at serious public health reform as a responsibility of good government.

ᴄᴏ 11 ᴏᴠ

BINDING UP THE
NATION'S WOUNDS

I n his second Inaugural Address on March 4, 1865, President Abraham Lincoln urged the North and the South "to bind up the nation's wounds."[1] When the Civil War ended a few weeks later, on April 9, the country began a slow period of recovery. During Reconstruction, however, another cholera epidemic struck. The medical war on this disease began anew; but this time the situation was different. In the years since 1849, when the last epidemic had occurred, common sense and science had come together to show the public and the medical world how cholera might at last be controlled.

Tests in England and Germany had proven without a doubt that cholera was passed from one person to another through contact with bodily excretions, such as vomit and fecal matter, from the ill person. It was finally understood that cholera came from a specific microorganism, yet to be determined, that was transmissible. The disease did not come from bad air or stardust, as some people once believed.

In October 1865 a ship docked in New York City Harbor. Sixty of its passengers were ill with cholera. The ship was not in quarantine, since it was now understood that quaran-

tines would not halt cholera anyway. Only sanitary reforms would. Freezing winter temperatures soon prevented the disease from taking hold on land since the microorganism either became dormant or died in cold weather. But everyone knew that when warm weather arrived the disease could decimate the population if something wasn't done about sewage contaminants and polluted water. In a city where pigs still helped to clean the streets, this new idea was a radical departure from the norm.

Civic-minded citizens and government leaders in New York were optimistic that winter, advocating a health-reform program that would bring an end to cholera epidemics. No one disagreed with their call for public health improvements, but it quickly became a political football and wasn't enacted into law until February. Once that happened, a Metropolitan Board of Health was again organized, and this time it worked. (Boards of Health had been previously attempted, but served only in emergencies.) For the first time, Americans in one city would successfully unite to fight off a health disaster.

Practical suggestions were put to work immediately, such as boiling water to disinfect clothing and bedding of the ill or dead. More cases of the disease broke out in April, but with the city cleaning up its streets and tenements as well as water and sanitation systems, only 591 deaths occurred in 1866. The epidemic turned out to be less than feared, but other cities without Boards of Health were not so fortunate. Once New York's success became known, other cities followed its example and formed health-reform boards and committees to literally clean up their acts.

Gradually, government was awakening to its responsibility in the area of public health. More states created boards, and, eventually, Congress would create a National Board of

Health in 1880 (but only to meet an emergency). After a yellow fever epidemic in the Mississippi River Valley in 1878, the federal government tried to establish a national quarantine against ships from tropical ports. Yet nothing was done about cleaning up the marshes and swamps that were the breeding grounds of the mosquitoes that carried yellow fever. After six years, the national board disbanded as local governments took more effective action.

American medical philosophy had undergone amazing changes during the thirty-four-year period since cholera had first invaded the nation. In 1832, cholera was considered a disease of the sinful. In 1849, medical practitioners knew it was caused by something specific, but they didn't know what. Now, in 1866, many physicians and an awakening public knew that cholera would respond to health reforms deemed crucial by new discoveries in science. Cholera's greatest contribution to American life would be an insistent reminder that there could be no public health without public sanitation.

After the Civil War, the nation's attention turned westward once again. For those soldiers whose lives in the East or South had been changed forever, or for those with a longing for new experiences and new horizons, there was only one way to go: west. The only lands that remained to be settled now were areas of the vast Great Plains. With conflicts between miners, Indians, ranchers, farmers, and townspeople—and the ever-present hostile weather—physicians would find much to do in this part of the country.

Among the people streaming westward were some whose only interest was in recapturing their health. In the early 1800s, tuberculosis had been the major cause of death in adults living in urban areas. As industrialization took hold, crowded living conditions resulted, and the number of tu-

*Doctors often advised their patients to go west and seek out sunshine
and fresh air to improve their health.*
(DENVER PUBLIC LIBRARY, WESTERN HISTORY DEPARTMENT)

cɔ⊙ ⊙ɔ

berculosis cases increased. Pioneers in rural areas were seldom affected, although a similar disease called scrofula usually kept pace with the settlers in their march west. Scrofula was a tubercular infection of the lymphatic glands that usually came from drinking the raw milk of infected cows. Most of the victims were children.

Tuberculosis, or consumption, as it was first called, had been a little-known health problem in the colonies. Accurate statistics were not kept, however, since tuberculosis was considered a family stigma. Those family members who had it were hidden away. Many physicians believed it was hereditary, too, since cases so often occurred in the same family.

Although tuberculosis was easy to diagnose in its advanced stages, its early symptoms of cough and change in body temperature could be confused with other diseases, so little was done to treat it. Once experiments showed that a specific germ was responsible and could be transmitted, Boards of Health around the nation went into action to isolate all TB cases in hospitals and sanitariums. As doctors began to recommend long, restful stays in fresh air and sunshine, tuberculosis sanitariums became common out west, especially in New Mexico, Arizona, and Colorado, where there was plenty of both.

Meanwhile, medical breakthroughs continued in Europe. In 1867, Joseph Lister, an English physician, published his paper on antiseptic surgery, giving both Pasteur and Semmelweis credit for laying the groundwork. Lister, too, blamed germs, or "disease dust," for spreading infection and advocated spraying carbolic acid over the patient during surgery to prevent infection. Carbolic acid, it was later discovered, was poisonous and affected everyone who came in contact with it, physicians and nurses as well as patients.

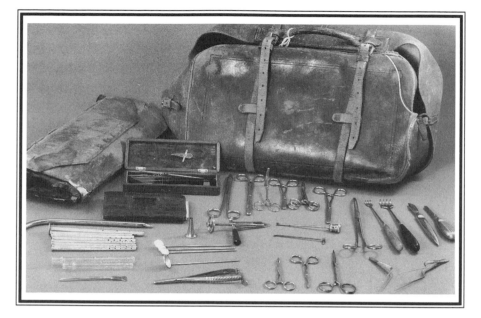

*A doctor's saddlebag of the late nineteenth century was large
enough to carry a variety of instruments, including a pronged
candleholder on the left, which could be wedged into a
wall to provide the physician with light.*
(STANFORD UNIVERSITY LANE MEDICAL CENTER)

Although Lister had the right idea, in 1887 the use of carbolic acid was abandoned, even by him, as an effective
method of antisepsis. By that time, however, other sterile
procedures had begun.

On the frontier, thoughts of antiseptic surgery were remote. Surgery was still an act of desperation, only resorted
to when there was no alternative. Equipment such as mallets,
probes, gouges, hooks, and knives weren't clean. Whiskey
was the anesthesia, and soap and water was the antiseptic, if
the patient was lucky. Amputations continued to be popular

solutions for many medical problems, and one newspaper reported that a certain local doctor had amputated twenty-two toes in three months.

When physicians were called out to emergencies, they had no way of knowing what to expect, so surgeries were often performed in unusual places: under cottonwood trees, in saloons or kitchens, carpentry shops, and wagon beds, for example. Members of the family helped hold the patient down and swatted flies while the doctor worked.

Sometimes the doctor was not only surgeon but dentist as well. One doctor had made dentures for a woman who failed to pay him. Later, when he asked to examine the dentures for a moment, he placed them in his pocket and said he would return her teeth when she paid for them. She did so and he returned her teeth.

The greatest obstacle to decent or even adequate medicine in much of the West was communication. Although the final spike of the transcontinental railroad had been driven home in 1869, joining the East and West coasts of the nation, it didn't connect isolated farms and villages. A doctor traveled by horse and buggy over great distances to reach a patient. He lacked decent medication and equipment, and often didn't hear about the latest scientific advances for months. Even then he was sometimes slow to accept it. Some frontier doctors continued the heroic practice of performing phlebotomy on a patient well into the mid-1800s.

Although vaccinations for smallpox were given in the West as early as 1801, the year after the procedure was introduced in the East, epidemics often erupted in isolated areas. At Fort Benton, Montana, in 1869, an epidemic of smallpox broke out when a steamer came up the Missouri River, bringing several men who were infected. After their deaths, Native Americans dug up their bodies for the clothing, and an entire tribe of Gros

Ventre Indians caught the disease. Of the 1,500 tribe members, 800 died. When the Native Americans placed their dead in trees, as was the custom of that tribe, traders came along and took their robes, spreading the disease even more.

Many settlers remained suspicious of vaccination and refused to have anything to do with it. In the closing years of the nineteenth century, Utah was hard hit by an outbreak of smallpox. Surrounding states complained and recommended to the federal government that vaccinations be made compulsory everywhere. Arguments followed that this was unconstitutional and, even worse, arms and legs would fall off if people were vaccinated. But no one reported a loss of either when the state of Utah proceeded with vaccinations.

Members of the Church of Jesus Christ of Latter-day Saints had settled much of Utah and believed they would stay well if they lived by the word of God, shunned liquor, tea, coffee, tobacco, and other vices. Brigham Young, leader of the Mormons, advocated the laying on of hands instead of calling the doctor and using mild herbs and foods that were known and understood by the members.

He had a tendency to look down on anyone who didn't earn a living by honest work and, in his mind, physicians fit this category. When a doctor wrote to him, offering to lead a group of converts from Illinois to Utah, Young told him he would be welcome if he wanted to earn his bread like an honorable man.

In the West, women's influence grew. Many Mormon women became successful midwives, making home remedies from native materials. Often their medical practices included more than obstetrics. Pauline Phelps Lyman, for example, covered the burned face of a little girl with linseed oil. The child recovered completely, without a scar.

Brigham Young apparently changed his mind about physicians and encouraged Ellis Reynolds Shipp to become more than a midwife. After she was married and the mother of four, she traveled east to the Woman's College of Pennsylvania and studied to become a doctor. Graduating in 1878, Dr. Shipp inspired her sister and her husband to become physicians also. Back in Salt Lake City, Dr. Shipp established her own Obstetrics and Nursing School, where she taught for many years. At the age of ninety-two, she said, "In a land renowned for its equal opportunities for women, it's amazing so few follow a profession so befitting them."[2]

Other women now pressured for more opportunity and recognition. Dr. Georgia Arbuckle Fix was a pioneer in medicine just by being a woman, but she also pioneered in settling the Great Plains. After she received her medical degree from the State University of Omaha's College of Medicine (she was the only woman in her class), Dr. Fix homesteaded a site on the North Platte River, near what is now Minatare, Nebraska. Often, she drove herself in a horse-drawn buggy to make house calls many miles from home. When she fell asleep on the way, her horse stopped at the right farm or ranch since they usually had been there before. If bad weather prevented her from going any farther in the buggy, she simply unhitched it and rode the horse the rest of the way.

One day, she was called to one of her most difficult cases and set out across the prairie to a distant farm. There she found the farmer had fractured his skull in an accident. Knowing she had to cover the portion of his exposed brain or he would die, Dr. Fix took a silver dollar from her purse, pounded it into a thin metal plate, and sewed it into the farmer's skull. She is credited with being the first physician to successfully perform this operation, becoming a pioneer in medical procedure as well.

Because of their isolation on ranches and farms, many

Dr. Georgia Arbuckle Fix (1852–1918) often filled the roles of dentist and preacher as well as physician in the remote area where she lived and worked near Minatare, Nebraska, during the westward expansion of the nation.

(NEBRASKA HISTORICAL SOCIETY)

*Horse-drawn wagons displaying ads for patent medicines were
part of the traveling medicine shows of the frontier days.*
(DENVER PUBLIC LIBRARY, WESTERN HISTORY DEPARTMENT)

settlers relied on themselves or succumbed to the lure of
"medicine men," the quacks who promised a cure for anything and everything. These salesmen promoted their "patent medicines" from town to town or in advertisements
placed in farmers' journals and almanacs. "Bill the Healer"
was typical of many. He traveled Wyoming in the 1870s to
sell his "magic" potion. His accomplice preceded him, going
into a saloon and pretending to become ill. Bill then appeared on the scene and miraculously cured him with his
bottle of elixir before moving on to the next town.

Other medicines, such as "King of Pain," were good for
baldness or deafness, or whatever problem the patient had.
"Colder's Liquid Beef Tonic" was sold as a cure for alcohol-

112

ism, yet its contents were over 26 percent alcohol. "Simmons Liver Regulator" was a remedy for everything, including "Disgust for Food and Prostration of the System." One of the best sellers in nineteenth-century records of patent medicines was "Dr. Miles's Compound Extract of Tomato," guaranteed to reach a patient's "weak" spot. Today it is known as ketchup.

Patent medicines and the pitchmen eventually developed into full-blown medicine shows with acrobats, elephants, and magic acts, traveling around the country to entertain a gullible audience before the "doctors" pitched their marvelous remedies to them. In one year alone, seventy-five million dollars was spent on patent medicines until state governments enacted legislation against dishonest claims by the manufacturers and salesmen.

But the legislation varied and, oftentimes, the pitchmen would simply move on to another state whose laws were less strict or less rigidly enforced. Not until 1906, when the Pure Food and Drug Act was passed by Congress, did more stringent laws become effective. However, manufacturers of bad medicine still found ways around it. Even today, a person looking for a magic cure will find one.

ɔ12ɑ

WE WILL ALWAYS
BE PIONEERS

In 1880 the United States had a population of fifty million people. It was rapidly becoming an economic giant among nations and struggling with labor problems and financial panics that were a part of growth and urbanization. Yet the majority of its citizens still lived on farms or in small towns and villages.

The world of medicine was similar. Science was taking giant steps along the path to medical enlightenment, turning cities into centers for innovative and lucrative practices. The country doctor, however, still practiced as a kindly friend to the family. The doctor knew everyone, from grandparent to baby, and treated them with all the drugs and tools available to him.

His doctor's bag probably included salicylic acid, which could reduce fever. Eventually, it would become the main ingredient in aspirin. He also had sugarcoated pills, often filled with his own vile-tasting concoctions, but still relied on opium, digitalis, quinine, and mercury, only in less lethal doses than before. Sulphur pills, thought to be effective against cholera, were new additions to his black bag. Some

*A doctor's black bag of the late nineteenth century, carried by a
nonsurgical, urban practitioner, contained many drugs of the
day plus diagnostic tools that were a blend of old and
new methods of treatment.*
(STANFORD UNIVERSITY LANE MEDICAL CENTER)

doctors even carried sulphur candies. Although the doctor's
hands, ears, and eyes were still his primary diagnostic tools,
he was aware that new scientific ones were available. He was
even agreeable to using some of them.

This was the beginning of the decade in which physicians everywhere became more interested in measuring a
patient's health through temperature, pulse, and blood pressure because much could be learned from these indicators.
Yet doctors still felt they weren't obtaining enough informa-

tion on the patient and demanded a more scientific approach. This, in turn, placed pressure on manufacturers to design even better and more reliable instruments.

Thermometers were in most doctors' black bags now. Although a form of the instrument had been introduced to the world as early as 1592 by Galileo, an Italian astronomer, it had no scale of numbers. Further variations of Galileo's model were extremely long and had to remain in the patient's mouth for as much as twenty-five minutes. Then, in 1717, a German physicist, G. D. Fahrenheit, substituted mercury for alcohol in the glass tube so that the thermometer became self-registering; that is, it did not have to be read while still in the patient's mouth. The earlier thermometers, without mercury, could not sustain a recorded temperature outside the patient's body. Fahrenheit also standardized the numbers to the scale used today. Now it became possible for someone else to take the temperature of a patient, and the accurate readings helped the doctor decide on a course of treatment.

Early Greeks realized the pulse was an indicator of health. For years, they tried to understand its rate, rhythm, strength, and regularity. Then, in the 1700s, a second hand on a watch was developed especially for doctors who wanted to time a patient's pulse rate. For more than fifty years afterward, only physicians wore watches with a second hand.

Before the stethoscope, the physician only had his ears to listen to a person's heartbeat and other body sounds. Then, in the early 1800s, a French physician named René Laënnec noticed some children at play, communicating through tapping sounds. It gave him the idea to roll up cylinders of paper and listen to his patient. He improved on this, and by 1817 had invented the first stethoscope, with wooden cylinders replacing the paper. The first binaural stethoscope—a stethoscope that delivers sound to both ears—was invented by Dr. George P. Camman in 1855. It consists of two earpieces connected to a listening bell which is held against the chest of a patient. Many internal disorders can be detected with this instrument.

Another important instrument was the ophthalmoscope, which allowed the physician to look directly into the interior of a patient's eyes. This device offered the doctor his first view of internal pathology. Introduced in the 1860s, it immediately became widely used, since it gave the doctor another tool with which to find conditions he was not able to discover externally.

Childbirth had never been considered a problem of health until this time. Since large families were needed to expand the nation's borders and frontier, children were thought of primarily as economic assets. Farmers and ranchers considered them annual crops along with the barley and corn, politicians regarded them as future votes, and religious leaders believed they followed naturally from the directive to "go forth and multiply." Women died at early ages owing to lack of health care during pregnancies and childbirth. A man usually needed several wives to deliver a quota of babies that would survive. In 1850, the death rate among children five years of age and younger was more than 21 percent.

The crude medical techniques relating to childbirth were slow to change at first. Obstetrical forceps had been used by doctors since the late eighteenth century to guide the baby's head through the birth canal. Even the frontier doctor had one forceps in his bag. But forceps wouldn't work when the baby's head was too big or when other complications arose. Then a difficult decision had to be made: Save the baby or save the mother.

Cesarean surgery (delivery of a baby by incision through the wall of the abdomen) was performed on dead women at first, in order to save the baby. Sometimes it was performed on live mothers who were going to die anyway. Surprisingly, some lived.

If the doctor decided to save the mother, he was forced to commit one of the cruelest procedures in medicine. He performed a fetal craniotomy, literally crushing the baby's skull in order to deliver it. Only in the late nineteenth century, when cesarean sections became reliable following the advances in antisepsis and anesthesia, could a doctor then save both mother and baby. Only then was childbirth a health-care concern.

The practice of obstetrics was not the only branch of medicine to experience medical advances. Transition was in the air in 1880 in all specialties. New concepts of the real nature of disease were being more readily accepted. Science was making physicians think beyond traditional treatment; the practice of heroics was seldom used now as newer drugs and surgical alternatives were considered.

Medical schools, licensing, and medical societies were directly affected by a more scientific approach to medicine. By 1880, there were one hundred medical schools in the nation. A handful were diploma mills that had few or no academic requirements for admission and required few skills for graduation. But as curricula expanded to answer the demands of scientific inquiry, those schools faded away. Teaching and training became more orderly, and clinical opportunities increased for interns and residents. Specialization was now more widespread, with training in Europe becoming popular again.

In this nation, the first school to require three years of

study was Harvard. Soon, other institutions followed its example. Next, all schools standardized courses and length of study. In 1881, the University of Pennsylvania's medical school became the first to require entrance exams.

Doctors were about to become respected citizens again. The general level of health of all settlers and respect for physicians on the frontier had improved enough that the Commission of Indian Affairs now required all doctors hired by them to have medical degrees.

The war continued against bacterial disease as more and more discoveries were announced. The first evidence that bacteria actually cause disease was revealed in 1876 by a German physicist, Robert Koch, when he showed that bacteria cause anthrax. Other discoveries quickly followed. In 1882, Koch isolated the specific bacillus that causes tuberculosis. The following year, during a scientific expedition to Egypt, he discovered the origin of cholera. It was an organism that he called *Vibrio comma,* a comma-shaped bacterium that finds its way into the human intestine because of polluted water, sewer contaminants, and poor hygiene. Dr. Daniel Drake, the midwestern pioneer, had been right, after all, when he said that dirty cities and people harbor cholera.

The bacillus for diphtheria was isolated in 1884, again by Koch, and an antitoxin was developed ten years later by him and Louis Pasteur. Public pressure mounted on Boards of Health to push doctors to use the antitoxin. As a result, the attention of the general population as well as the medical community now became focused on solving bacterial problems.

Yellow fever had been one of the worst diseases to plague the United States, killing thousands annually. Several theories had been put forward to explain its origin. With the

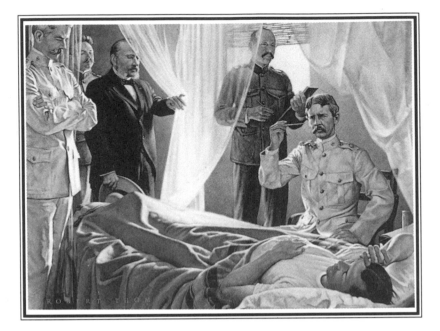

In an uncultivated field in Cuba, Dr. Walter Reed set up Camp
Lazear where he successfully carried out experiments on army
personnel volunteers to win the war against yellow fever.
Another hero in the fight against the disease was
Dr. William Crawford Gorgas, standing left.
(PARKE-DAVIS, A DIVISION OF WALTER-LAMBERT COMPANY)

෴

advances in bacteriology, it was hoped that its bacterium
might be discovered and could be eradicated.

Dr. Walter Reed had another theory, however. He
thought it was transmitted by mosquitoes. In a series of experiments he carried out with army volunteers, he proved
that the disease came from a virus injected into the blood-
stream by an infected mosquito, the *Aedes aegypti*. Yellow
fever became the first human disease credited to a virus.

The frontier was rolling back, geographically and scientifically. On the Great Plains, trained physicians replaced Indian medicine men. Sometimes, the trained physicians were Native Americans who were college-educated in the white man's schools, then returned to temporarily replace the shamans of their ancestors. Among them were Dr. T. J. Bond, a Choctaw Indian; Dr. Carlos Montezuma, an Apache; and a Santee Sioux named Dr. Charles A. Eastman. Dr. Eastman was present to see the results of the massacre at Wounded Knee Creek in South Dakota, on December 29, 1890. He described the bloodbath as "a severe ordeal for one who had so lately put all his faith in the Christian love and lofty ideals of the white man."[1]

The battle at Wounded Knee was the last armed conflict between the U.S. Army and Native Americans. The ghost dance that had predicted Indian victory was but a memory as Native Americans were rounded up for reservations, their lives irrevocably changed.

Life on the western frontier had changed forever. After settlers claimed the last remaining land in the Great Plains, the director of the census announced in 1890 that "there can hardly be said to be a frontier line"[2] in the United States. The geographic frontier was gone.

However, the medical frontier continues to expand as civilization moves toward the twenty-first century. Discoveries in new fields and rediscoveries of old methods point the way to better health and longer lives. For instance, leech therapy is making a comeback as a method to prevent blood congestion and encourage healing. (Those in the medical field can now order leeches by dialing an 800 number.) Although scourges such as smallpox and diphtheria have nearly been wiped out, much remains to be done. Diseases such as AIDS and cancer, and the return of tuberculosis, challenge medical science. Many answers continue to remain just beyond our grasp. Perhaps, in the words of a long-ago frontier physician, "we [still] know nothing definitely."[3] Perhaps the medical frontier is only beginning, and we will always be pioneers.

∾ Notes ∾

1 · OLD MEDICINE COMES TO THE NEW LAND

1. Carl J. Pfeiffer, *The Art and Practice of Western Medicine in the 19th Century* (Jefferson, N.C.: McFarland, 1985), p. 103.
2. David and Elizabeth Armstrong, *The Great American Medicine Show* (New York: Prentice Hall, 1991), p. 17.
3. Wilbur R. Jacobs, *Dispossessing the American Indian* (Norman, Okla.: University of Oklahoma Press, 1985), p. 163.
4. Ibid. p. 163.
5. Ibid. p. 163.
6. Armstrong, *The Great American Medicine Show*, p. 4.

2 · DISEASE HEADS WEST

1. Dorothy Fisk, *Dr. Jenner of Berkeley* (Kingswood, Surrey: Windmill Press, 1959), p. 113.
2. Cotton Mather, *The Angel of Bethesda* (Barre, Mass.: Barre Publishers, 1972), p. 99.
3. John Duffy, *Epidemics in Colonial America* (Baton Rouge, La.: Louisiana State University Press, 1953), p. 133.
4. Whitfield J. Bell, Jr., *John Morgan, Continental Doctor* (Philadelphia: University of Pennsylvania Press, 1965), p. 109.
5. Ibid. p. 7.
6. Howard R. Hauser, *Wilderness Doctor, the Life and Times of Dr. John Hole* (Centerville, Ohio: Centerville Historical Society, 1980), p. 5.
7. Morris H. Saffron, *Surgeon to Washington* (New York: Columbia University Press, 1977), p. 44.
8. James O. Breeden, ed., *Medicine in the West* (Manhattan, Kans.: Kansas Sunflower University Press, 1982), p. 5.

123

9. Benjamin Rush, *Essays, Literary, Moral and Philosophical* (Philadelphia: Bradford Press, 1806), p. 213.

3 · New Methods, No Cures

1. Madge E. Pickard and R. Carlyle Buley, *The Midwest Pioneer* (Crawfordsville, Ind.: R. E. Banta, 1945), p. 86.

2. U.S. Bureau of Census, *Historical Statistics of U.S., 1789–1945* (Washington, D.C.: Government Printing Office, 1949), p. 25.

3. Ibid. p. 25.

4. Carl J. Pfeiffer, *The Art and Practice of Western Medicine in the 19th Century* (Jefferson, N.C.: McFarland, 1985), p. 111.

5. Bernard DeVoto, *The Journals of Lewis and Clark* (Boston: Houghton Mifflin, 1953), p. 21.

6. Ibid. p. 445.

7. Ibid. p. 80.

8. Ibid. p. 182.

9. David and Elizabeth Armstrong, *The Great American Medicine Show* (New York: Prentice Hall, 1991), pp. 7–8.

4 · No Ounce of Prevention Here

1. James H. Cassedy, *Medicine and American Growth, 1800–1860* (Madison: University of Wisconsin Press, 1986), p. 17.

2. Wilbur R. Jacobs, *Dispossessing the American Indian* (Norman, Okla.: University of Oklahoma Press, 1985), p. 29.

3. Madge E. Pickard and R. Carlyle Buley, *The Midwest Pioneer* (Crawfordsville, Ind.: R. E. Banta, 1945), p. 11.

4. Ibid. p. 13.

5. Ibid. p. 16.

5 · Along Came Cholera

1. Charles E. Rosenberg, *The Cholera Years* (Chicago: University of Chicago Press, 1962), p. 161.

2. Carl J. Pfeiffer, *The Art and Practice of Western Medicine in the 19th Century* (Jefferson, N.C.: McFarland, 1985), p. 112.

3. William G. Rothstein, *American Physicians in the 19th Century* (Baltimore: Johns Hopkins University Press, 1972), p. 35.

4. Rosenberg, *The Cholera Years*, p. 30.

5. David and Elizabeth Armstrong, *The Great American Medicine Show* (New York: Prentice Hall, 1991).

6. Ibid. p. 55.

6 · THE SPECIALISTS TAKE OVER

1. James Flexner, *Doctors on Horseback* (New York: Dover Publications, 1937; reprinted 1969), p. 166.

2. Ibid. p. 165.

3. Madge E. Pickard and R. Carlyle Buley, *The Midwest Pioneer* (Crawfordsville, Ind.: R. E. Banta, 1945), p. 15.

4. Daniel J. Boorstin, *The Americans: The Colonial Experience* (New York: Vantage Books, 1958), p. 42.

5. David and Elizabeth Armstrong, *The Great American Medicine Show* (New York: Prentice Hall, 1991), p. 82.

6. Ibid. p. 81.

7. Pickard and Buley, *The Midwest Pioneer*, p. 67.

8. Ibid. p. 67.

9. James O. Breeden, ed., *Medicine in the West* (Manhattan, Kans.: Kansas Sunflower University Press, 1982), p. 7.

7 · TRAUMA ON THE TRAIL

1. Thomas B. Bell, *Medicine on the Santa Fe Trail* (Dayton: Morningside Bookshop, 1971), p. 82.

2. Ibid. p. 2.

8 · THE ART OF HEALING

1. George W. Groh, *Gold Fever* (New York: William Morrow, 1966), p. 33.

2. Georgia W. Read, "Diseases, Drugs, and Doctors on the Oregon Trail in the Gold Rush Years," *Missouri State Historical Society,* vol. 38 (1944), pp. 260–76.

3. Groh, *Gold Fever,* p. 176.

9 · Doctors Wanted: No Women Need Apply

1. Ralph Jackson, *Doctors and Diseases in the Roman Empire* (London: British Museum Press, 1988), p. 86.

2. Laurel Thatcher Ulrich, *A Midwife's Tale: The Life of Martha Ballard* (New York: Vintage Books, 1991), p. 12.

3. Ibid. p. 50.

4. Ibid. p. 354.

5. Ibid. p. 358.

6. Ruth Abrams, ed., *Women Doctors in America* (New York: Norton, 1985), p. 44.

7. Ibid.

8. Ibid. p. 93.

9. Ibid. p. 62.

10. Ibid. p. 63.

11. Ulrich, *A Midwife's Tale,* p. 348.

10 · When Beans Killed More Men Than Bullets

1. George W. Adams, *Doctors in Blue* (New York: Henry Schuman, 1952), p. 208.

2. Ibid. p. 208.

3. Ibid. p. 16.

4. Laurann Figg and Jane Farrell-Beck, "Amputations in the Civil War: Physical and Social Dimensions," *Journal of the History of Medicine,* no. 4 (October 1993).

11 · Binding Up the Nation's Wounds

1. Stephen B. Oates, *With Malice Toward None* (New York: Harper and Row, 1977), p. 411.

2. Western Writers of America, *Women Who Made the West* (New York: Avon Books, 1980), p. 162.

12 · WE WILL ALWAYS BE PIONEERS

1. Robert F. Karolevitz, *Doctors of the Old West* (Seattle: Superior Publishing, 1967), p. 17.

2. *World Book Encyclopedia*, Chicago: Scott Fetzger, 1988 edition, vol. 21.

3. Madge E. Pickard and R. Carlyle Buley, *The Midwest Pioneer* (Crawfordsville, Ind.: R. E. Banta, 1945).

✦ Glossary ✦

Abscess—The collection of a bacterial infection in the form of pus in a localized area of the body, which often becomes swollen and inflamed.

Ague—An expression used for fever or shaking, chills, pains in the bones and joints, etc., which came to be used to describe malaria in frontier times.

Anthrax—An infectious disease of cows, sheep, and other mammals, including man, marked by a carbuncle, caused by the *Bacillus anthracis*.

Antisepsis—Arresting, or stopping, of bacteria that cause infection.

Antitoxin—A substance formed in the body, usually from immunization, that counteracts a specific toxin.

Argonauts—A group of mythological heroes who traveled by ship in search of treasure. The gold miners who traveled by ship to California were named after them.

Asepsis—The medical process of excluding bacteria from a surgical area.

Bacteria—Single-celled microscopic organisms, usually classified with plants. Larger than viruses, not all bacteria are harmful.

Basswood—An herb used for medicinal purposes.

Bromine—A chemical element used as a sedative at one time.

Cadaver—A dead body.

Calomel—Mercury chloride, formerly used as a laxative, later discovered to be poisonous.

Camphor—A chemical used to repel insects, and to treat infections, pain, and itching.

Carbolic acid—One of the first antiseptics to be used by Joseph Lister; later discontinued after it was discovered to be poisonous.

Choler—Anger, irritability, wrath.

Cholera—An acute bacterial disease caused by *Vibrio comma*, with diarrhea, vomiting, and cramps.

Conjunctivitis—Inflammation of the conjunctiva, or thin membrane that covers the exposed portion of the eyeball.

Craniotomy—An operation in which the skull is opened, usually to operate on the brain.

Croup—A condition, usually caused by a virus infection, where the larynx or trachea is obstructed, causing a dry, harsh cough and difficulty in breathing. This is usually found in children.

Dengue—An infectious fever of warm climates, with severe pain in the joints and muscles.

Digitalis—A preparation made from dried leaves of the foxglove plant, used originally by Indians and later by doctors to treat heart disease.

Diphtheria—A severe infection affecting upper respiratory passages, caused by *Corynebacterium diphtheriae*, where a membrane forms in air passages, especially the throat, obstructing breathing.

Dissection—Cutting apart during surgery or to study the structure or anatomy of the body.

Diuretics—Substances that increase the flow of urine.

Dock root—An herb used for medicinal purposes.

Dysentery—An infection that causes inflammation of the lower bowel, resulting in diarrhea that becomes bloody mucus, and abdominal pain.

Eclectic—A sect of medicine that draws its theories from all the others.

Emetics—Drugs that cause vomiting.

Empirics—Doctors who based their knowledge on information gathered from experience rather than from books.

Endemic—Disease that is unique to a locality, like a tropical fever.

Epidemics—Diseases that affect many people at the same time in the same place and spread from one person to another.

Epilepsy—A disorder of the nervous system, causing episodes of convulsions that may end in unconsciousness.

Erysipelas—An infection of the skin and underlying tissues now known to be caused by group A Streptococci.

Gangrene—Death of body tissue owing to inadequate blood supply.

Homeopathy—A system of alternative medicine developed by Samuel Hahnemann, a German physician.

Hypochondria—An emotional condition marked by depression and imaginary ill health.

Immunization—The process of developing the body's resistance to disease, which happens either by having the disease and developing a natural immunity to it or by injection of immunoglobulins.

Influenza—An acute and highly contagious infection, caused by a virus, that usually affects respiratory organs.

Inoculation—The introduction of bacteria or viruses into the body to prevent disease.

Intermittent fever—Another name for malaria.

Ipecac—A small plant of South America whose dried roots are used to induce vomiting.

Lancet—A small, two-edged surgical knife, formerly used for opening abscesses or in bloodletting.

Laudanum—Tincture of opium, formerly used for deadening pain.

Leech—A bloodsucking worm that attaches itself to the skin. It was formerly used in bloodletting, for it secretes hirudin, a substance that prevents blood clotting.

Malaria—A disease caused by infection carried by the *Anopheles* mosquito.

Miasma—Noxious exhalations from decaying organic matter, which were formerly believed to infect the atmosphere.

Microorganism—A microscopic plant or animal.

Midwife—A woman who assists women in childbirth.

Neuralgia—A sharp pain along a nerve.

Obesity—The condition of being exceptionally fat.

Ophthalmoscope—An instrument for viewing the interior of the eye.

Organism—Any form of plant or animal life.

Patent medicine—Medicine sold without prescription from a doctor. During frontier days, such medicines were advertised as having been patented, but few were.

Pesthouse—House or building where people ill with contagious diseases could be kept to isolate them from the well population.

Phlebotomy—The practice of opening a vein for bloodletting, used as a remedy for an illness.

Phlegm—The mucus in the respiratory passages.

Pleurisy—Inflammation of the membrane covering the lungs and interior wall of the chest, caused by infection.

Pneumonia—Inflammation of the lungs caused by microorganisms.

Poultice—A soft, damp mixture spread on a cloth and applied to the body for healing.

Preceptor—A teacher or mentor.

Puerperal fever—An infection during and right after childbirth, also called childbed fever, caused by a group A *Streptococcus* microorganism.

Purgative—A medicine that purges, or cleans, by causing evacuation of the bowels.

Quack—A slang term for an unlicensed or unscrupulous medical practitioner.

Quartan—Malarial fever recurring at seventy-two-hour intervals.

Quinine—An alkaloid made from the bark of the cinchona tree.

Quinsy—An abscess, occurring as a result of an acute infection of the tonsils.

Renaissance—The revival of learning and art beginning in fourteenth-century Italy and continuing through Europe into the seventeenth century.

Rheumatism—A term loosely applied to aches and inflammations of the joints that cause stiffness and problems in locomotion.

Saffron—An herb, or condiment, used for medicinal purposes, now used for cooking also.

Salve—A soothing ointment for the skin.

Scarlet fever—An infection from group A *streptococcus pyogenes*, usually of the throat, accompanied by a skin rash, fever, and vomiting.

Sciatica—Pain along the sciatic nerve, focusing sensation to the back of the thigh and outer side of the leg and foot.

Scrofula—A tubercular disease that causes swelling and degeneration of the lymph glands, especially in the neck, and inflammation of the joints.

Scurvy—A disease caused by vitamin C deficiency, with swollen and bleeding gums.

Shaman—A Native American medicine man or woman.

Sitz bath—A small tub or basin of lukewarm water, sometimes with Epsom salts dissolved in it, in which a patient sits to relieve rectal, colon, or rheumatic problems.

Stethoscope—An instrument through which a physician listens to interior sounds of the body, primarily of the lungs and heart.

Streptococcus—A microorganism that causes many diseases in humans. It is killed by heat and disinfectants, and it is controlled by antibiotics, usually of the penicillin family.

Tertian—A malarial-type fever with attacks that occur every other day.

Tuberculosis—A disease caused by *Bacterium tuberculosis*, once called consumption, that can affect many parts of the body, but most often the lungs.

Typhoid fever—A disease caused by *Salmonella typhi*, usually transmitted through food or water when conditions are less than sanitary, causing intestinal inflammation and ulceration.

Typhus—An acute infection caused by *Rickettsia prowazekii*, spread by lice and fleas.

Vaccination—Introduction of bacteria and viruses to develop immunity and prevent disease.

Virus—A microorganism so small that it cannot be seen under the light microscope. It lives inside the host cell and has to use the host's resources to multiply.

Yaws—A chronic disease of the tropics caused by *Treponema pertenue*, causing skin eruptions.

Yellow fever—An acute infectious disease caused by a virus carried by the mosquito *Aedes aegypti*, causing jaundice, vomiting, hemorrhages, etc.

৻৩ Bibliography ৶৵

Books

Adams, George W. *Doctors in Blue*. New York: Henry Schuman, 1952.

Abrams, Ruth, ed. *Women Doctors in America, 1835–1920*. New York: Norton, 1985.

Adams, Samuel Hopkins. *The Erie Canal*. New York: Random House, 1953.

Andrist, Ralph K. *The Erie Canal*. New York: American Heritage, 1964.

Armstrong, David, and Elizabeth Armstrong. *The Great American Medicine Show*. New York: Prentice Hall, 1991.

Baxby, Derrick. *Jenner's Smallpox Vaccine*. London: Heinemann Educational Books, 1981.

Bell, Thomas B. *Medicine on the Santa Fe Trail*. Dayton: Morningside Book Shop, 1971.

Bell, Whitfield J., Jr. *John Morgan, Continental Doctor*. Philadelphia: University of Pennsylvania Press, 1965.

Boorstin, Daniel J. *The Americans: The Colonial Experience*. New York: Vantage Books, 1958.

Breeden, James O., ed. *Medicine in the West*. Manhattan, Kans.: Sunflower University Press, 1982.

Cassedy, James H. *Medicine and American Growth, 1800–1860*. Madison: University of Wisconsin Press, 1986.

Cayleff, Susan E. *Wash and Be Healed*. Philadelphia: Temple University Press, 1987.

Cunningham, Andrew, and Roger French. *The Medical Enlightenment of the 18th Century*. Cambridge: Cambridge University Press, 1990.

DeVoto, Bernard. *The Journals of Lewis and Clark.* Boston: Houghton Mifflin, 1953.

Duffy, John. *Epidemics in Colonial America.* Baton Rouge: Louisiana State University Press, 1953.

Fisk, Dorothy. *Dr. Jenner of Berkeley.* Kingswood, Surrey: Windmill Press, 1959.

Flexner, James. *Doctors on Horseback.* New York: Dover Publications, 1937; reprinted 1969.

Groh, George W. *Gold Fever.* New York: William Morrow, 1966.

Hall, Thomas B., M.D. *Medicine on the Santa Fe Trail.* Dayton, Ohio: Morningside Bookshop, 1971.

Hauser, Howard R. *Wilderness Doctor, the Life and Times of Dr. John Hole.* Centerville, Ohio: Centerville Historical Society, 1980.

Hendrick, Willene, and George Hendrick, ed. *On the Illinois Frontier.* Carbondale and Edwardville, Ill.: Southern Illinois University Press, 1981.

Jackson, Ralph. *Doctors and Diseases in the Roman Empire.* London: British Museum Press, 1988.

Jacobs, Wilbur R. *Dispossessing the American Indian.* Norman, Okla.: University of Oklahoma Press, 1985.

Karolevitz, Robert F. *Doctors of the Old West.* Seattle: Superior Publishing, 1967.

King, Lester M., M.D. *The Medical World of the 18th Century.* Chicago: University of Chicago Press, 1958.

Mather, Cotton. *The Angel of Bethesda.* Barre, Mass.: Barre Publishers, 1972.

Oates, Stephen B. *With Malice Toward None.* New York: Harper and Row, 1977.

Pfeiffer, Carl J. *The Art and Practice of Western Medicine in the 19th Century.* Jefferson, N.C.: McFarland, 1985.

Pickard, Madge E., and R. Carlyle Buley. *The Midwest Pioneer.* Crawfordsville, Ind.: R. E. Banta, 1945.

Read, Dr. George Willis. *A Pioneer of 1850.* Boston: Little, Brown, 1927.

Rister, C. C. *Southern Plainsmen.* Norman, Okla.: University of Oklahoma Press, 1938.

Rosenberg, Charles E. *The Cholera Years.* Chicago: University of Chicago Press, 1962.

Rothstein, William G. *American Physicians in the 19th Century.* Baltimore: Johns Hopkins University Press, 1972.

Rush, Benjamin. *Essays, Literary, Moral and Philosophical.* Philadelphia: Bradford Press, 1806.

Saffron, Morris H. *Surgeon to Washington.* New York: Columbia University Press, 1977.

Savitt, Todd L., and James Harvey Young. *Disease and Distinctiveness in the American South.* Knoxville: University of Tennessee Press, 1988.

Shyrock, Richard Harrison. *Medicine and Society in America, 1660–1860.* New York: New York University Press, 1960.

Smillie, Wilson G. *Public Health: Its Promise for the Future.* New York: Macmillan, 1955.

Steiner, Paul E. *Disease in the Civil War.* Springfield, Ill.: Charles C. Thomas, 1968.

Stewart, George R. *The California Trail.* New York: McGraw-Hill, 1962.

Stone, Eric. *Medicine Among the American Indians.* New York: Paul Hoeber, 1932.

Studt, Ward B; Jerold G. Sorensen; and Beverly Burge. *Medicine in the Intermountain West.* Salt Lake City: Olympus Publishing, 1976.

Ulrich, Laurel Thatcher. *A Midwife's Tale: The Life of Martha Ballard.* New York: Vintage Books, 1991.

U.S. Bureau of Census. *Historical Statistics of the U.S., 1789–1945.* Washington, D.C.: 1949.

Wolfson, Evelyn. *From the Earth to Beyond the Sky.* Boston: Houghton Mifflin, 1993.

Western Writers of America. *Women Who Made the West.* New York: Avon Books, 1980.

ARTICLES

Figg, Laurann, and Jane Farrell-Beck. "Amputations in the Civil War: Physical and Social Dimension." *Journal of the History of Medicine and Allied Science,* vol. 48, no. 4 (October 1993).

Read, Georgia W. "Diseases, Drugs, and Doctors on the Oregon

Trail in the Gold Rush Years." Missouri Historical Society, vol. 38 (1944).

DISSERTATION

Jochims, Larry. "Medicine in Kansas, 1850–1900," Part 2. Emporia, Kansas: Emporia State University, 1981.

✤ Index ✤